Abundant Lives

Abundant Lives

A Progressive Christian Ethic of Flourishing

Amanda Udis-Kessler

The Pilgrim Press, 1300 East 9th Street
Cleveland, Ohio 44114
thepilgrimpress.com

Published 2024.

Printed on acid-free paper.

Library of Congress Cataloging-in-Publication Data on file.
LCCN: 2023945582

ISBN 978-0-8298-0057-9 (paper)
ISBN 978-0-8298-0058-6 (ebook)

Printed in the United States of America.

Contents

I acknowledge that the city of Colorado Springs, Colorado, where I live, is the homeland and unceded historic territory of many Native American Nations. The Nuuchiu ("the People"), or the Utes, are the longest continuous Indigenous inhabitants of what is now Colorado.

I also acknowledge that land acknowledgements mean nothing if we are not working for justice for, and for the flourishing of, Native American and other Indigenous people today. I commit to donating 50% of all royalties from Abundant Lives *to One Nation Walking Together (https://www.onenationwt.org/), an organization supporting Native Americans in the Rocky Mountain region of the United States and beyond, in perpetuity. I encourage all readers to make similar locally or regionally appropriate commitments as they are able.*

I dedicate this book to all people, of any religion or no religion, who strive to live in ways that support the flourishing of all people and of the planet. The world is better for each of you.

Foreword

Once upon a time, barge workers labored to transport a heavy bronze bell up a river in China. Not quite balanced on the barge, the bell slipped out of its cradle and sank into the inky black waters of the river. Experts debated. Engineers were consulted. But despite every attempt to recover the valuable bell, none succeeded.

One day, a clever monk came along and was told of the situation. He asked for permission to try and retrieve the bell himself—provided that, if successful, the bell would be given to his monastery. Since at this point any effort seemed hopeless, the owners agreed that he could try.

The monk gathered as many volunteers as he could and set them to work collecting bamboo poles. He then hired divers to take the poles down one by one and fasten them to the bell (no easy task considering the light and practically unsinkable characteristics of bamboo).

Long after people had lost count of how many poles were fastened to the bell, a diver popped to the surface and enthusiastically reported that he thought the bell had moved ever-so-slightly. Then, when the next pole was added, the accumulated buoyancy of all the poles shifted the bell in the mud, broke the riverbed's hold, and lifted the enormous bell to the surface. With ropes attached, the bell was hauled to shore, wrestled onto a cart, and installed at the monastery's temple where it still resides today.

Friends, like our proverbial bell, Jesus's clarion call to new life has today become hopelessly mired in the mud and muck of the swirling waters of what passes for Christianity. Mainline churches are in hospice mode, exvangelicals are denouncing the whole enterprise while beating a path to atheism, and fundamentalists are doubling down on moral outrage, misogyny, and fearmongering.

It's time for a renewed ethic of love—all the while embracing the profoundly biblical (but long-dormant) aspiration of collective human flourishing. In *Abundant Lives: A Progressive Christian Ethic of Flourishing*, Amanda Udis-Kessler takes us on a transformative journey and invites us to embrace a profound paradigm shift.

As an advocate for a more comprehensive understanding of our shared human experience, Amanda invites us to recognize the interconnectedness of all individuals and social groups, empathize with the lived experience of those who are different from us, and seek ways to foster a sense of unity that transcends the superficial boundaries of our differences. This, she argues, is the clearest path forward in achieving the vision of that particular "kin-dom" that finds its roots in Hebrew scripture and its Christian expression in the teachings of Jesus.

Who exactly is this Amanda Udis-Kessler character and what qualifies her to speak of an ethic that transcends our existing status quo? A sociologist, social ethicist, and theologian by training, Amanda also brings lessons learned through her personal journey from secular Judaism through Unitarian Universalism to progressive Christianity and brings her strengths as a prolific writer and gifted musician to the envisioning of a new focus for twenty-first-century Jesus followers.

As a fellow writer, I have been more than a little envious of Amanda's virtually spontaneous expression of complex ideas into relatable, understandable prose. As a fellow musician, I not only admire the objective breadth of Amanda's musical gifts (both as a composer and as a lyricist) but have experienced the impact her music has on congregations in the midst of a variety of gatherings. (I commend to you Amanda's website and its ever-expanding collection of original music for free use in your setting: https://queersacredmusic.com.) And as an aspiring theologian, I am grateful for the example of Amanda's articulate and inspiring conveyance of deep wisdom in fresh and generative language.

Amanda's rich background offers just the kind of energy contemporary progressive Christianity needs: a collective vision that all of us can embrace. Amanda grounds her ethic of flourishing in Jesus's greatest teachings: stop obsessing over principles and practices for their own sake! Practice love by prioritizing the tangible and intangible needs of others, especially the most vulnerable among us. Love even enemies, working to support their wellbeing.

Imagine, she asks, if we were to confront the pervasive forms of inequality that hinder the flourishing of marginalized groups.

Imagine if we were to actively engage in dismantling the barriers to establishing a just and equitable society.

Imagine if we were to preface every conversation, every task, every policy decision with the question, "What will increase the joy and decrease the pain?"

Imagine if we were to reflect on our own lives and assess the profound impact our choices and actions have on not only our well-being but especially the well-being of others.

Considering the self-inflicted battering conventional Christianity continues to bring upon itself, it's easy for those of us who remain to become discouraged. We may think our contribution to any effort at salvaging Jesus's ethic of love is too small or insignificant to make any difference. But like individual poles of bamboo, each of our efforts brings its own unique buoyancy to the overall effort. Each of us may not be able to accomplish ALL of the work needed to be done, but each of us can become agents of flourishing according to our own gifts and in our own settings.

The cleverest of wily monks, Amanda not only asks us to *imagine* this new world of abundance, following Jesus's call to courageously practice generosity, vulnerability, and humility—she lays out the plans. *Abundant Lives: A Progressive Christian Ethic of Flourishing* is a comprehensive guide to living into the life of meaning, compassion, and love you've been looking for.

May the wisdom that follows herein inspire you to a renewed appreciation for the gift of your own being, a commitment to the flourishing of others, and nurture a deep sense of connection to and responsibility towards the well-being of all of creation. With our accumulated efforts at promoting an ethic of flourishing, there's no telling what bell we can raise!

Rev. David M. Felten
Pastor, The Fountains United Methodist Church
co-author, Living the Questions,
June 20, 2023

Introduction

They shall all sit under their own vines and under their own fig trees, and no one shall make them afraid.
(Micah 4:4a)

Dream God's dream. Holy Spirit, help us dream
Of a world where there is justice and where everyone is free
To build and grow and love and to simply have enough.
The world will change when we dream God's dream.
(Bryan Sirchio, "Dream God's Dream")

In November 2022, an antigay, anti-trans shooter targeted Club Q, an LGBTQ+ nightclub in my city. Five people were killed and twenty-five injured. It's a nightmare that happens over and over and over again in the United States—hundreds of times in 2022 alone ("List of Mass Shootings," n.d.). Broken-hearted, I went to the memorial that had been set up in front of the club where the shooting took place to see how people were responding to the violence. I was not sure what to expect, but I was hoping for a few flowers and maybe a sign or two.

Instead, I found hundreds of flowers and candles, dozens of stuffed animals, signs and balloons and Pride flags running the length of a city block, a magnificent riot of color. One sign read, “Hate has no home here.” Another sign read, “We stand with our LGBTQIA+ Community.” A third sign read, simply, “Faith. Hope. Love.” Memorial posts had been put up for the five people who had been killed; each post had a heart on it on which people had written notes. Chalk was available for mourners and the sidewalk near the memorial was covered in chalked messages: “God loves you.” “We care.” “Hate is evil. Love endures forever.”

As I arrived, I saw a mother hand her young daughter a bouquet of flowers, instructing her to put them with the other flowers near a Pride flag. A man wearing a politically progressive t-shirt explained to a local news reporter that it was important for heterosexual people to be present in support of the Club Q community. Some people wept loudly; others offered quiet words of consolation. There were easily fifty people there when I arrived, and another twenty made their way over as I left. To say that the tragedy and beauty of humanity was on full display sounds clichéd, yet I cannot think of a better way to describe the experience.

Our world is full of pain and joy, violence and creativity, cruelty and kindness. How should we live? What should our actions be? We make decisions about who to be and what to do, minute by minute, day by day, lifetime by lifetime. What wisdom, what hope, what courage should guide those decisions? How shall we respond to the good we encounter? To the evil? These are ethical, moral questions, some of the most important questions we can ask given the unspeakable good and the terrifying evil around us—and of which we ourselves are capable.

One answer might be that we should respond with love, but that answer only raises more questions. What does love look like in our day and time? How can we love ourselves, other people and the God of our understanding in ways that make a positive difference in a magnificent and struggling world? How can those of us who seek to follow Jesus do so in a way that embodies and brings to life his dream of a world of peace and joy in which everyone has what they need?

In this book, I attempt to answer both sets of questions—the classic ethical questions about how to live a moral life and the urgent contemporary questions about how we can embody and enact love in a world desperately in need of it. My answer to both sets of questions is the same:

> **We should commit ourselves to living out an ethic of flourishing in which our values, actions, and social institutions are centered on helping all people to have good lives and on minimizing the avoidable suffering that makes people's lives harder.**

This answer is neither simple nor obvious, and I will spend the next seven chapters clarifying what I mean and indicating how we might move toward living out this commitment.

Most approaches to ethics focus on principles or abstract values such as justice, freedom, duty, or virtue, often using hypothetical situations to make their claims. In contrast, my approach puts people ahead of principles. As I'll discuss in chapter 1, principles and abstract ideas can be used for ill as well as for good, to harm as well as to help. If our goal is for all people to have the opportunity to have good lives, we must understand even our most cherished principles, ideas, values, and beliefs not as ultimate goals, but as the way we reach the ultimate goal: a world in which all people have a real chance to flourish.

In such a world, to recall progressive Christian songwriter Bryan Sirchio's words from the epigraph, there would be justice and everyone would be free to build and grow and love and to simply have enough. And in such a world, to paraphrase the words of the prophet Micah, no one would need to be afraid because no one would need to harm anyone else. In such a world, mass shootings such as the one at Club Q would be a thing of the past. Can you imagine living in such a world? I can, and it is stunningly beautiful. Would it not be worth the considerable effort it will take us all, individually and collectively, to draw closer to a world in which all people—and ultimately perhaps all beings—have the opportunity to thrive? I believe that it would be worth the effort, which is why I wrote this book. Humanity can move toward a world of human flourishing if we understand the steps we need to take and the work to which we are invited. This book introduces us to some of those steps and to some of that work.

A Progressive Christian Ethic

The dream of a world of human well-being is not specific to any one religious tradition or indeed to religious people. Humanist traditions, for example, hold values that contribute to human flourishing when lived out thoughtfully. I believe that the ideas in part 1 will appeal to a wide range of people of many religious traditions and none. At the same time, because these ideas align particularly well with progressive Christianity, part 2 of the book connects the claims and ideas of part 1 with the biblical tradition and with contemporary progressive Christian thought.

Progressive Christianity receives much less media coverage than its conservative and evangelical counterparts, so I should say what I mean by this term. Progressive Christians can be understood as people who:

> Believe that following the way and teachings of Jesus can lead to experiencing sacredness, wholeness, and unity of all life, even as we recognize that the Spirit moves in beneficial ways in many faith traditions; seek community that is inclusive of all people, honoring differences in theological perspective, age, race, sexual orientation, gender identity/expression, class, or ability; strive for peace and justice among all people, knowing that behaving with compassion and selfless love towards one another is the fullest expression of what we believe; embrace the insights of contemporary science and strive to protect the Earth and ensure its integrity and sustainability [and] commit to a path of life-long learning, believing there is more value in questioning than in absolutes. (ProgressiveChristianity.org 2022)

The chorus of Bryan Sirchio's song "Dream God's Dream" suggests that God's dream is a world of human and planetary flourishing. When Jesus referred to the "Kingdom of God" or the "Kingdom of Heaven" (as the terms are translated in the Gospels), he was, I believe, envisioning a realm of flourishing. Theologian Ada Maria Isasi-Diaz refers to this vision as the "kin-dom of God" (Bass 2021) and Rev. Dr. Martin Luther King, Jr. called it the "beloved community" (Tatter 2019). Whatever we call it, it is a vision of abundant lives for all people and potentially for non-human living beings. Moreover, Jesus's invitation to love God, ourselves, our neighbors, and our enemies can be understood as a call to work for our own flourishing, the flourishing of others, and the flourishing of non-human creation.

Ultimately, I invite those of us who find Jesus's vision compelling to take up an ethic of flourishing as a way of responding to the good news of Jesus today. Sirchio writes, "the world will change if we dream God's dream," and I believe that sentiment. Perhaps, if enough people believe it, we can make it so.

Thinking about Flourishing

I first thought about the importance of flourishing in a secular context, informed by my sociology training, my leftist feminism, and my identity and experiences as a queer (bisexual) androgynous white woman who strives to work against white supremacy. I studied ethics as part of my undergraduate religion major and found my way back to it later in life. However, the more I read, the more frustrated I became with the standard approaches. As a sociologist, I got impatient with ethics based on abstract principles such as justice rather than on insights about what people are actually like and what we actually need to live well. I also felt that the standard approaches gave far too much positive weight to the power of rational thinking. Rationality has been a mixed blessing for humanity, contributing both to our greatest accomplishments and to our most astonishing cruelty. Moreover, as a politically progressive feminist and queer person, I felt that most ethical theories were oddly lacking in a dedicated focus on human well-being. What, I wondered, is the point of ethics if not to help all people flourish?

More broadly, this book has been decades in the making. Personal experiences of sexism and heterosexism combined over time with my growing understanding of how I benefit from white supremacy on a daily basis to shape my political commitments. Studying comparative religion in college, sociology in graduate school, and religion again in seminary helped me think about the power of meaning systems, including religion, for good and ill. My spiritual journey from secular Judaism to Unitarian Universalism to, more recently, the progressive wing of the United Church of Christ, has provided an additional venue for my deep passion to alleviate suffering and expand human flourishing. I enter into the Christian story as a non-doctrinal universalist besotted by Jesus's vision of human well-being and striving to do my part to make it a reality. The ideas and claims here bring together my political commitments, sociological perspective, moral concerns, religious studies, and spiritual journey.

Plan of the Book

Part 1, "Human Flourishing," lays out my core ethical approach without reference to religious perspectives. In chapter 1, "From Principles to People," I claim that basing ethics on principles or values is problematic and propose instead a focus on human flourishing, expanding my description of flourishing from that provided in this introduction. Chapter 1 also introduces the idea of avoidable suffering as an experience that can limit or damage flourishing.

In chapter 2, "Our Common Humanity," I discuss ten universal attributes of what it means to be a human being. Specifically, human beings are embodied, emotional, relational, meaning-making, agentic, learning, societal, moral (and immoral), creative, and spiritual (not necessarily religious) beings. While people are individuals and members of social groups as well as human beings, the universal attributes discussed in this chapter represent core aspects of our humanity common to all individuals and to members of all social groups. I also indicate what flourishing and avoidable suffering looks like in terms of each attribute and consider what "integrated flourishing" and "aggravated suffering" look like across attributes.

In chapter 3, "Flourishing, Suffering, and Inequality," I discuss ways in which systemic forms of inequality such as white supremacy and sexism lead to members of valued groups having more opportunities to flourish while members of devalued groups face more suffering that would be avoidable if not for the inequality itself. A commitment to flourishing, I claim, is a commitment to working against all forms of systemic inequality.

Because part 1 does not tie ethics to progressive Christianity or any other religious tradition, it may be of interest to secular people or people in religions other than Christianity.

Part 2, "The Kin-dom of God as a Community of Flourishing," connects the claims and ideas of part 1 with the biblical tradition and contemporary progressive Christian thought.[1]

In chapter 4, "Jesus, the Prophets, and Beyond," I draw on biblical materials to suggest that Jesus's understanding of the kin-dom of God offers a program that supports human flourishing, that Jesus's program emerged from the prophetic Jewish tradition that informed his thinking, and that his earliest followers were similarly concerned with flourishing, especially for the poorest and least protected among them.

In chapter 5, "Love, Flourishing, and God," I draw on selected biblical and contemporary progressive Christian understandings of God, love, and the relationship between them to propose a concrete, flourishing-centered approach to loving God, ourselves, our neighbors, and our enemies. I claim that loving ourselves means attending to our own

---

1 I use "kin-dom of God" instead of Jesus's term "Kingdom of Heaven" (changed by Luke to "Kingdom of God"). Jesus lived in an age of kingdoms and counterposed the (peaceful, abundant) kingdom of the holy to the (violent, exploitative) kingdom of Caesar. Today, we might counterpose the inclusive kin-dom (or community) of God to the exclusive communities of mistrust, fear, loathing, and greed that surround and tempt us.

flourishing and working to minimize our avoidable suffering, while loving our neighbors and enemies means working for their flourishing and against their avoidable suffering. Loving God means attending to the flourishing of human and non-human creation and working to mitigate avoidable suffering across creation. Working for flourishing and against suffering involves concrete actions focused on the core attributes of humanity discussed in part 1.

In chapter 6, "Co-Creating the Kin-dom of God: Our Individual Work," I consider the importance of engaging in psychological healing work, spiritual formation, and the development of such virtues as humility, compassion, courage, and generosity to enhance our ability to support flourishing and work against avoidable suffering—both in our own lives and in our broader actions for justice.

In chapter 7, "Co-Creating the Kin-dom of God: Our Collective Work," I consider the implications of the rest of the book for our justice work and suggest some ways in which our congregations can commit to becoming generous, hospitable communities of flourishing that support our larger work for human well-being.

The conclusion asks us to imagine a world of flourishing and invites us to begin or continue our work toward making that vision a reality.

I close with theologian Kurt Struckmeyer's "Creed of Love" and include as an appendix a set of questions suitable for book group discussions.

Some Cautions

Abundant Lives offers what I hope is a broadly accessible approach to ethics that has a universal sensibility while being grounded in specific experiences and situations, similar to Joseph Fletcher's (1966) situationist ethics but with more concrete guidance about what love might look like in practice. An ethic of flourishing can help us make decisions ranging from mundane daily choices to rethinking how large-scale social institutions (from religion to the economy to the government) could work more humanely.

All ethical approaches come with potential risks, and the universal sensibility in my approach—the idea that this approach could theoretically be used to address almost any ethical situation—brings a particular kind of risk. Especially when white, well-off, educated people in countries like the United States of America propose ethical approaches, we need to be careful that our universalizing approaches, however well-intentioned, do not silence or devalue people with different moralities.[2] So, I want to say clearly that my approach to ethics is not intended to override other approaches. An ethic of flourishing will not necessarily be appealing to people with sufficiently different starting assumptions than mine or to people in societies with substantially different cultures. I offer this approach to ethics as one possible way to engage with the moral demands and opportunities before us, and as one possible way to respond to the invitation of Jesus.

Finally, if you are reading this book from outside the United States of America, I apologize for how U.S.-centric the examples are. I have always lived in the United States and am most familiar with its culture and struggles. I hope the ideas and claims I offer will translate easily to your location, setting, and context. I hope even more that other people will continue to develop these ideas from within their own situations in ways that allow whatever may be valuable here to resonate far beyond the specifics of my life and hopes.

Let's get started.

---

2 Thanks to Rev. Dr. Christopher Grundy for pointing out this issue.

Part 1:
Human Flourishing

1

From Principles to People

Every moral action should have in view a concrete living person and not the abstract good. (Nicolas Berdyaev, The Destiny of Man *[sic], 1960, 106)*

Love is for people, not for principles...it is personal – and therefore, when the impersonal universal conflicts with the personal particular, the latter prevails in situation ethics. (Joseph Fletcher, Situation Ethics, *1966, 31)*

In 2014, I read an open letter by a United States right-wing media personality written in response to yet another mass shooting.[1] The letter was intended for the parents of the young people killed in the shooting. At one point in the letter, the man wrote, "as harsh as this sounds, your

1 I'm aware that this is my second mention of mass shootings in a book that is not primarily about mass shootings. Unfortunately, given the ubiquity of mass shootings in the United States and the ways in which they cause harm while pointing to larger problems in our society, they are an appropriate example in both places where I have mentioned them.

dead kids don't trump my constitutional [gun] rights" (NBC News 2014). That sentence stopped me in my tracks. It was so obviously ethically wrong. Everything about it was heartbreaking. At the same time, I had to acknowledge that it followed from the power and centrality that rights are accorded in the United States.

Rights are important, of course. People need access to certain rights if they hope to have a decent life. But rights are not a simple matter. Rights can be used for good or for ill, to support human flourishing or to cause unnecessary, avoidable human suffering. This is especially true when rights as defined for one group of people limit rights for other groups. Gun rights benefit US gun manufacturers and gun owners, for example, but in the absence of thoughtful and well-enforced gun safety laws, such rights contribute to thousands of injuries and deaths in the United States every year (BBC 2023) and rob US Americans of the right to safety. Antiabortion activists appeal to the "right to life" in ways that restrict women's reproductive rights. The US Supreme Court recently ruled that the religious rights of conservative people of faith trump the rights of LGBTQ+ people to service in some commercial venues (Liptak and VanSickle 2023). When we consider the range of situations in which people rely on rights language, it's clear that rights in and of themselves are not inherently a moral good. They can be used to help or to harm. Moreover, whether rights are experienced as helpful or harmful depends on whose rights are being upheld, whose rights are being overridden, and which rights are in question.

The same can be said of freedom as a value. In 2014, North Carolina Republican and US Representative Robert Pittenger argued that government should not interfere with businesses that fire employees for being gay because getting to fire someone strictly for their sexuality is one of "the freedoms we enjoy" (Clawson 2014). Pittenger did not answer the question of whether the freedom of getting to work at a job of our choosing, for which we are well qualified, and without the fear of being fired for irrelevant reasons, is another one of the "freedoms we enjoy." Since 2014, of the many proposed laws in the United States that include the word "freedom" in their titles, some expand freedom for all citizens while others restrict freedom for members of devalued social groups, including Black/Indigenous/People of Color (BIPOC) communities, women, and LGBTQ+ people. Even free speech is not inherently a moral good: it can be used either to lift up the voices and concerns of previously silenced people or to promote hatred and terror.

If neither rights nor freedom are consistently used for the good, what is the point of having them in the first place? This question, at least, is easy to answer. Our rights guarantee us certain freedoms, and we cannot make the lives we would choose for ourselves without those freedoms. Life without rights or freedom is not what we would consider a good life.

Some people make the argument that our rights should guarantee us access to certain social resources. President Franklin Delano Roosevelt famously declared that the United States needed a "second bill of rights" that included (among other things) rights to useful and well-paying jobs, decent homes, adequate medical care, and a good education ("Second Bill of Rights," n.d.). Why do we need access to these social goods? Because they allow us to maximize our likelihood of having good lives. Without access to work, housing, education, and medical care we cannot flourish.[2]

---

2 Economist Mark Paul (2023) has recently revisited Roosevelt's bill of rights for our time, covering the right to a good job at a living wage, safe and affordable housing, free education from pre-kindergarten through college, a healthy environment, quality

Beyond rights and freedom, many people focus on justice and equality as important ethical and political values. We can, however, ask the same questions about these values that we ask about rights and freedom. As noted above, "rights" language can be used to give some people rights and take away the rights of others, while "freedom" language can similarly be used to grant or remove freedom. Therefore, when we think about justice and equality, we want to know who is defining what "justice" or "equality" means in a given situation. We also want to know who benefits and who suffers from those definitions. However much we care about justice and equality in the abstract, we care even more about how they are used to help or hurt people.

We get angry about injustice and inequality because principles we value are being disrespected. I do not want to ignore the importance of that anger, but it is not the whole story. It does not explain all of our anger, and for me, it does not explain the most poignant part of our anger. We also get angry about injustice and inequality because they harm—and sometimes kill—living, breathing people. They stifle joy, limit creativity, and cause pain. To the extent that our anger about injustice and inequality has to do with the harm they cause, we already care about human flourishing whether we use that term or not. In the rest of this chapter, I begin to lay out an approach to ethics that has human flourishing at its heart.

By flourishing, I mean *getting to have a good life.* A flourishing life is not free of pain or difficulties, but it is also filled with joy, satisfaction, accomplishment, and contribution to the well-being of others. In such a life,

---

healthcare decoupled from employment, and access to a basic income and banking services. Paul argues that these rights can be based on the idea of freedom as access to those necessities of life that enable the "pursuit of happiness."

we experience abundance, delight, meaning, fullness, and wholeness; our joy and gratitude then lead us to work toward the same thriving for other people and for the planet. Flourishing humanity is humanity at its best, and we can take the fullest advantage of our human capabilities when we flourish.

Because people are complicated and flourishing can take many forms, a focus on flourishing has an aspirational quality. While it would be ideal to flourish across as many aspects of our lives as possible, that's often not realistic. Most of us flourish in some ways but not in others. For example, perhaps I'm in really good physical shape and I can use my body to help other people and enjoy myself, in which case I might be flourishing in my body. At the same time, maybe I have psychological struggles that make it hard to flourish emotionally. Alternately, maybe I'm happy most of the time and able to weather the daily ebb and flow of my emotions pretty successfully, but I have painful arthritis in my knees that limits what I can do physically.

Because of our complexity as human beings, we might flourish across some but not all of our core attributes. We can, nonetheless, work to lift up human well-being as broadly as possible—not just in our own lives but in the lives of all people. That is the nature of aspirations: they invite us to strive for them, whether we realize them completely or not. After all, more joy is always better than less joy. More gratitude is a good thing. The ability to contribute more fully to the well-being of others is a worthy goal. Focusing on human flourishing is a way to live out our love for ourselves and others.

Prioritizing human well-being does not mean that we ignore the importance of rights, freedom, equality, justice, and other principles and values. It means, rather, that *we treat people, rather than principles, as the point of ethics.*

People flourish and suffer; principles and values do not. People rejoice and weep; laws and material things do not. In 1996, President Clinton signed the Defense of Marriage Act, which restricted marriage to heterosexual couples; in 2022, President Biden signed the Respect for Marriage Act, which overturned the earlier law and protected same-sex and interracial marriage to some degree. To state the obvious: Marriage doesn't care what happens to it; however, people care whether they can get married or not because the ability to marry legally carries many rights and benefits. Those rights and benefits, along with the social support that comes with them, contribute to human well-being. Marriage is a complex matter and being married legally does not inherently guarantee flourishing; but being unable to marry one's beloved legally can make life harder in many ways (Bedick 1997). Marriage exists for humanity; humanity does not exist for marriage. If marriage can help people flourish and if we care about human well-being, marriage should be as widely available as possible.

If people are the point of ethics, we need an ethical approach that starts and ends with valuing people and supporting human well-being, not with abstract principles or values. To work toward developing that approach, let's consider a second definition of flourishing which is a bit more focused than the one I introduced above:

> **People flourish when we are encouraged and enabled to be and to become our whole best selves, to fulfill our potential, to contribute effectively to the well-being of others and to society more broadly, and to live joyful, meaningful lives that make a difference and leave a legacy.**

I've already referred to suffering in relation to flourishing and will say more about their connection later in the chapter, but for now we also need a preliminary definition of avoidable (unnecessary) suffering. Here is a first pass:

> **Avoidable suffering is the suffering that results from discomfort, pain, harm, or danger[3] that people would not need to face if society were organized in ways that allowed all people to flourish. Avoidable suffering thus results from situations that limit, block, or damage flourishing in its fullness.**

With those preliminary definitions in place, here's a claim with which we might begin generating an ethic of flourishing:

> **All people, without exception, ought to have the opportunity to flourish and to avoid unnecessary suffering.[4]**

A humane approach to ethics begins with this claim rather than with a claim based on abstract principles and values such as rights, freedom, equality, or justice that can

---

3 Chapters 2 and 3 address specific types of discomfort, pain, harm, and danger more directly. Examples might include food or housing insecurity, experiences of sexual or other physical violence, and discrimination in education, hiring, or treatment by the criminal justice system.

4 The "without exception" clause may trouble people. Most of us agree that there are actions people can take (such as raping or murdering someone) that call for a response that might limit the flourishing of the person carrying out the attack. My claim here is based on the idea that there is nothing *inherent* about people for which they should be excluded from the opportunity to flourish. The consequences of their behaviors may be another matter.

be used to cause suffering as well as flourishing. We can move on to make the following claims:

> **Morally good ideas, principles, values, beliefs, actions, cultural norms, organizations and large-scale social institutions are those that support human flourishing—both our own flourishing and that of all other people.**
>
> **Morally problematic ideas, principles, values, beliefs, actions, cultural norms, organizations, and large-scale social institutions are those that block human well-being or that contribute to otherwise avoidable suffering.**

These claims allow us to evaluate the morality of specific ideas, principles, and actions based on their consequences: Do they lead to flourishing or to suffering, and for whom? We can ask these questions about any and every aspect of our lives from our smallest daily decisions and actions to our religious organizations, economic systems, and other institutions in society.

An ethic of flourishing does not approach rights as the final goal. Rights are, rather, a way to reach the goal of human well-being. Rights used to promote human well-being are a moral good; rights used to cause human suffering are a moral problem. Rights are morally neutral until put into practice and can be put into practice in beneficial or detrimental ways. The same could be said of all other moral and political principles, and indeed of the many concepts, practices, and organizations that make up society.

This approach to ethics, while conceptually straightforward, is complicated in practice. It's one thing to claim that human flourishing is a moral good and that avoidable human suffering is a moral problem. What, however, does that mean on a day-to-day basis? How does this claim provide guidance for our actions or for the way society is organized? How do we live morally and help others live morally when moral living is centered on human well-being? We will turn to these questions shortly, but first I need to say a little more about suffering.

Author Dorothy Allison (1994, 36) writes, "I grew up poor, hated, the victim of physical, emotional, and sexual violence, and I know that suffering does not ennoble. It destroys." The kind of suffering Allison describes here is what I call "avoidable suffering," and it differs from the unavoidable suffering we find bound up with flourishing.

When we love someone and they become sick or die, we suffer. We worry about their sickness; we are filled with grief at their passing. When a cherished relationship comes to an end, we mourn our loss. Such suffering is painful and hard, sometimes devastating. The pain, however, comes directly from our flourishing. Loving other people is a source of joy and losing them is a source of pain. This is not a pain most of us want to avoid. However difficult the loss of loved ones, the alternative would be refusing to love people.

Similarly, the process of emotional healing from prior trauma or psychological harm can be profoundly uncomfortable, involving its own kind of suffering. This suffering, however, can lead to greater flourishing over time: greater joy, greater courage, greater resilience.

In contrast, the poverty, hatred, and violence described by Dorothy Allison cause avoidable suffering. Such suffering results from situations that limit human well-being and cause harm. These situations include all forms of systemic inequality, unregulated capitalism, and any other circumstance that withholds the resources we need to flourish or puts us in danger's way. The resources we can't access might be material, financial, emotional, social, or a combination; the danger we face might be physical, psychological, or both. Regardless, when such circumstances keep us from being and becoming our whole best selves, fulfilling our potential, contributing effectively to society, and living joyful, meaningful lives, we suffer.

Such suffering is avoidable because it is often the result of how society is organized; if we made changes in laws, culture or both, some of this suffering would never come to pass. For example, consider how changing US gun laws and culture might limit avoidable suffering. If guns were harder to access and gun safety laws were more stringently enforced, there would be fewer shootings and therefore fewer gun-related injuries and deaths. If society made it harder for even one potential mass shooter to obtain guns, some people would live who will otherwise die of gun violence. Each person spared death by shooting would continue to offer the world their beauty and kindness, their creativity and cleverness, their spiritual wisdom (and perhaps their terrible puns, though not everyone would find those such a gift). Maybe such a person would find a cure for cancer, write the great pop music hit of 2030, or otherwise make a substantial contribution to society. Even if they simply lived a quiet life, however, their living would spare the suffering of their friends, family, and loved ones who would not need to grieve their tragic, unnecessary death.

Avoidable suffering operates at individual levels as well as group levels, with mental health providing a good example of how the levels intersect. Societies with economic, cultural and social stressors that exacerbate mental health challenges while not making high-quality mental health support available to all people can expect avoidable mental health suffering across all sectors of society. At the same time, societies with any form of systemic inequality can expect members of devalued, mistreated groups to experience additional unnecessary mental health stressors as a result of the emotional pain and fear that come with being disbelieved, mistrusted, and discriminated against. In a society with both large-scale stressors and systemic inequality, even members of socially valued groups may suffer needlessly while members of devalued groups will suffer even more.

Based on the above points, it is possible to add another claim to our ethic of flourishing:

> **We can and should work to limit or end avoidable suffering, both our own and that of others. Working against individual and societal avoidable suffering is a moral priority just as working to expand human flourishing is a moral priority.**

How, then, shall we use these broad ideas about flourishing and suffering to help us understand what our concrete priorities should be? Individuals and groups of people have different values and priorities, after all. How can we claim to know what someone else wants or needs?

An answer—not the only answer, but my answer—is to begin with some basic, universally agreed upon and non-controversial attributes of humanity. We may not know every detail about every individual, but we do know certain things about what it means to be a person. We know, for example, that all people, as human beings, share certain characteristics and traits, capacities and needs. I've chosen some attributes of humanity with which I think no one could reasonably disagree. These attributes make us who we are as human beings. Our individual and cultural experiences with these attributes differ, but all of them describe all people to at least some degree:

> We are embodied, physical beings.
>
> We are emotional, feelings-driven beings.
>
> We are relational beings who are both dependent on and interdependent with others.
>
> We are meaning-making beings who need to make sense of our experiences and our lives. Telling stories is a key way in which we make meaning.
>
> We are agentic beings, which is to say that we have self-efficacy and the need to act on and have an impact on the world around us.
>
> We are learning beings who grow and develop over the course of our lives.
>
> We are societal beings, meaning that our lives are interwoven with the larger societies of which we are a part.
>
> We are moral beings, and sometimes immoral beings.
>
> We are creative beings, given both to making new things and to appreciating the creativity of others.
>
> We are spiritual beings, meaning that we can experience awe, reverence, wonder, and a sense of being part of something larger than ourselves.

Our spirituality can be tied to organized religion, but it does not need to be.

It's important to bear in mind that enumerating these attributes of humanity separately is artificial. We are always embodied and always emotional and always relational and so on. The reason to separate out each attribute is to understand how it is part of our humanity and what implications it has for our flourishing and suffering. As it turns out, we do not merely flourish and suffer as individuals or even as members of social groups; we flourish and suffer as embodied beings, emotional beings, relational beings, and in the context of the other attributes listed above.

Once we bring the lofty language of flourishing down to the specifics of human attributes, we begin to understand concrete ways in which we can contribute to our own flourishing and to the flourishing of others, both people we know and people we do not know. We also move toward identifying concrete ways to work against our own suffering and the suffering of others. In chapter 2, I consider these attributes more closely.

2

Our Common Humanity

[T]he solution to the suffering and oppression that has undoubtedly emanated from homophobic—as well as racist and sexist—understandings of what it means to be human is not to give up altogether on the concept of the human being as a source for normative values and ethical judgments [but instead] to present and defend a more convincing and non-oppressive conception of what it means to be human and to lead a fully human life. (Carlos Ball, The Morality of Gay Rights, *2003, 10)*

In chapter 1, I suggested that we should understand human beings as having a complex set of attributes such as embodiment, emotions, and creativity (among others) through which we flourish and suffer. In this chapter, I take us through these attributes in a little more detail, focusing on their importance for our lives.

Before we turn to those attributes, there's one more aspect of human complexity to consider. You might object to my focus on universal human attributes by pointing out that you are an individual with your own unique set of experiences, stories, and understandings of the world.

And you would be right. We are all individuals and our individual perspectives are important. You also might object that even if all people share certain human attributes, we belong to different social groups and may have very different life experiences based on whether the groups we belong to are treated well in society. If you pointed this out, you would also be right. Our race, gender, socioeconomic status, sexuality, and other identities impact our experiences profoundly. For example, white people do not get pulled over by the police for "driving while white" but members of BIPOC communities are routinely pulled over for "driving while Black or Brown." Similarly, men and heterosexual people rarely need to worry that their rights (specifically as men and as heterosexual people) will be on the ballot at election time or will be overruled by the US Supreme Court; women and LGBTQ+ people worry about these issues and with good reason.

Just as we are always embodied beings *and* emotional beings *and* relational beings in addition to the other attributes discussed here, we are also always simultaneously individuals *and* members of social groups *and* human beings with shared traits, capacities, and challenges. All three of these elements of humanity are always in play for us, but may be more or less salient in different situations. As I write these words, I'm particularly aware of my individuality: when the US Supreme Court overturned Roe v. Wade, I was acutely aware of being female in a sexist society. That said, I am always both an individual and a member of a devalued social group based on my gender.

People can also simultaneously flourish and suffer as individuals or as members of groups. For example, the mention of arthritic knees in chapter 1 was a real-life example: my arthritic knees do in fact limit my physical flourishing to some extent. At the same time, the luck of growing up with a songwriter father has facilitated my creative flourishing as a hymnwriter and sacred music composer. My whiteness makes it easier for me to flourish in a white supremacist society, while my gender and sexual identities leave me at greater risk for suffering in a sexist, heterosexist society. That said, the particular ways in which I—and everyone—will flourish and suffer come back to those basic human attributes. It is time to consider them at greater length.

Embodied Beings

We are embodied, physical beings.

Our embodiment is among the most basic things about us. We live our lives in and through our bodies, suffer when our bodies suffer, and die when our bodies give out or if they are harmed badly enough. The extent to which we are identified with our bodies led Christian ethicist James Nelson (1978, 20) to refer to people as "body-selves."

Our bodies are not merely the limiting factor of whether we are healthy (or alive) or not; they are themselves a venue of well-being, pleasure, and agency. The range of things we can do with our bodies is amazing. Through them we experience the comfort and connection of touch—in sexual intimacy, hugging a friend, or snuggling a pet. We experience a sense of accomplishment when we play an instrument, climb a mountain, or win a basketball game. We lose ourselves in dancing to a favorite song or singing in a chorus. When we labor at our jobs, take care of our children, or run errands, we use our bodies; when we work out or practice a sport, we strengthen and train them.

At the same time, our bodies are vulnerable. We may become sick or get injured, perhaps even permanently. We may have physical disabilities that limit us, especially if we live in societies (like the United States) that do not prioritize expanding options for people with disabilities.

The lovely connection of voluntary human touch can become traumatizing when touch is unwanted or violent. Individual violence, or collective violence such as war, can permanently damage or destroy our bodies. The harm we do to our environment will, sooner or later, show up on and in our bodies, whether through zoonotic diseases that we catch from animals displaced due to development projects, or through the droughts, flooding, and dangerously high temperatures that accompany global climate change.

It's not only our own lives that are bound up with our bodies, however. We help others flourish or cause others to suffer based on words we say and actions we take using our bodies. We create and birth the next generation of people with and through our bodies. The aforementioned damage to our environment comes from choices we make and live out in our embodiment; if we are to mitigate global climate change, we will have to do it by changing what we do with our bodies and how we treat them. Our bodies are a central part of our humanity. Our embodied flourishing and suffering is a high-stakes matter.

As *embodied* beings, we flourish when we use our bodies for empowerment, accomplishment, and delight in work, play, creativity, or other venues. We flourish when we experience "pleasure, joy, and at home-ness in our bodies" (Ellison 1996, 14). We also flourish when we connect with other people and non-human beings through our bodies.

We suffer when a lack of access to survival resources or quality healthcare leads to illness, injury or death. We suffer when we experience physical or sexual violence or other types of avoidable harm, such as injuries that happen at insufficiently regulated workplaces. We suffer when we face trauma or emotional stressors so profound as to cause wear and tear to our bodies. We suffer when our ability to use our bodies for efficacy and enjoyment is limited due to laws or cultural practices that restrict our bodily autonomy.

Emotional Beings

We are emotional, feelings-driven beings.

If getting through the day depends on our bodies, what the day is like depends on our emotions, feelings, and moods. Across all of our diversities, we likely agree that a good day includes some positive emotions such as happiness, and that a day full of sadness, anger, or fear could have gone better.

We feel emotions in our bodies—the relaxation of joy, the clenched gut of fear, the tight throat or ticklish nose that precedes a good cry. Positive emotions can energize us while negative emotions can be exhausting. Moreover, our emotions are connected to our memories through our senses: the smell of a favorite childhood food can evoke tender feelings of joy, grief, or both, while hearing that song we associate with our first teenage breakup can remind us of the sadness that accompanied that breakup.

Our emotions are also bound up with how we understand the world. We are angry, sad, worried, or happy *about* something. Our emotions provide clues about what we think is going well or badly in our lives or in society around us. For example, we might be angry about something that does not seem to affect us directly, as when other people are discriminated against or mistreated. In this case, our emotions tell us something about our moral values. If we are angry that other people face discrimination, it is because we find discrimination unfair. Our anger is a protest about how things are, a wish for how things could be.

As *emotional* beings, we flourish when our lives are full of experiences and relationships that bring us happiness, delight, joy, and other positive emotions. We flourish when we experience and release our negative emotions without responding to them in self-destructive or otherwise destructive ways.

We suffer when we are not free or able to live our emotional lives fully. We suffer when circumstances force us to fear for our well-being or survival and when we experience discrimination, violence, or other kinds of harm that have emotional effects. We suffer when we cannot access the mental health resources we need, or when mental health challenges are stigmatized, making us too ashamed to access those mental health resources even if they are available to us.

Relational Beings

We are relational beings who are both dependent on and interdependent with others.

Another key attribute of our humanity is our relationality, encompassing our need for other people, their need for us, and our interconnectedness within a larger web of relationships. As John Pavlovitz writes: "Whether we find belonging in the context of houses of faith, in our neighborhoods, in political groups, or in online communities, we are wired for meaningful relationships" (2018, 204). While independence and autonomy are important to us as individuals, we also are inextricably interwoven with other people and our lives are bound up with theirs. We need to belong, to be part of families and groups and communities—to love and be loved.

While many of us do not like to think of ourselves as dependent on others, the reality is that we rely on them throughout our lives and they on us. We depend on others for the resources that allow our bodies to survive and thrive, for the information and stories and rituals that help us make sense of the world, for the companionship that allows us to feel connected, for the laws and rules and norms that allow us to get through each day. We rely on others to take care of us in our first and last moments of life, to teach us how to navigate society, to grow our food, to build our houses, to tend to our illnesses, and to infuse our lives with meaning, richness, and joy. Others similarly rely on us.

In fact, we depend on others before we are born and after we die. We depend on our birth or adoptive parents to imagine a world with us in it, anticipating and planning for our arrival, and we depend on our birth parents to stay healthy and keep us healthy before our birth. We depend on our friends, family, and other loved ones to remember us after we die and to keep us alive in those memories. Our dependence on others thus extends past the boundaries of our lives.

We are also interdependent with others in ways that go beyond our mutual dependence on one another. What we do impacts others, and what others do impacts us. To put it sociologically, we create and recreate society with each other, one interaction at a time. We make reality what it is, minute by minute and year by year, in the most mundane and amazing of ways. For example, we conspire collectively to drive safely—that is, interdependently—and most of the time, we succeed. We elect candidates that share our values through communal get-out-the-vote campaigns. We sing in a choir or play in a band or orchestra; our contribution joins that of others to make a final, beautiful product that is more than the sum of its parts.

Our interdependence can, of course, harm as well as heal and destroy as well as create. An army is as interdependent as an orchestra. A hate mob is as communal as a political campaign group. It matters what we do with our interdependence. But the fact of our interdependence is undeniable—as is our dependence, as is our independence.

As *relational beings,* we flourish when we establish meaningful relationships with family members, friends, colleagues, and others, when we cherish others and are cherished by them, and when we belong to larger communities. We flourish when we receive the care and support that we need from others and when we are part of the collective work of building a just and joyful society.

We suffer when we are shunned, isolated, cut off, or otherwise kept from meaningful relationships. We suffer when we are not welcome in communities that are important to us. We suffer when we do not receive the care we need and we suffer when we are prevented from working interdependently with others to build the world we seek.

Meaning-Making Beings

We are meaning-making beings who need to make sense of our experiences and our lives. Telling stories is a key way in which we make meaning.

As little as I know about the first human beings, I am fairly sure of one thing: They did not sit around the fire after a hard day of gathering and hunting and quote statistics. Instead, they told stories. Then, their descendants told stories—stories that developed into culture, that solidified into religions, that provided guidance and warnings, that set expectations about what was right and wrong, possible and impossible. Humanity has always told stories, stories that enabled us to live good lives and stories that constrained us to suffer. We told stories that inspired us to help others and stories that justified killing others.

Today, when we gather around the fire, over a hot drink in a café, or in front of the Zoom screen, we still tell stories. When we try to make sense of our lives, when we fend off fear, when we seek comfort or connection with others, we tell stories. We tell stories to mourn, to organize, to celebrate. We tell stories that empower us to create and stories that legitimize destruction.

Stories help us understand who we are, why we are here, what we believe in, and what we reject. Stories teach us what the world is about and how it works. We are born into a world of stories, growing up with stories in our families and our schools and our religious communities. When we become adults we pass our stories along to the next generation, knowing that they will do the same. Over time our stories become our memories, solidifying our identities, values, and interests.

Humans are story-telling beings because we are meaning-making beings. Stories help us organize and convey information, connect with others, learn (and teach) lessons, and otherwise make sense of a complicated and often frightening world. Stories are part of larger meaning systems that include rules, laws, social norms, and other understandings that help us navigate our experiences. We receive far more sensory information on a daily basis than we can process, and we cannot respond to any of this information unless we can interpret it. Our meaning systems give us the information and tools to do that interpreting, shaping how we respond to our experiences and thus how we act in the world.

Just as stories can help as well as harm, our meaning systems more broadly impact our flourishing and suffering because they guide us in what to value and in what to do, both as individuals and as communities. How we interpret reality has profound consequences for us and others, indeed for the planet.

For example, as pastor and author Brian McLaren (2022, part 1) points out, Christianity as a meaning system has been antisemitic, violent even to its own dissidents let alone to "infidels," colonialist, racist, patriarchal, hetero-sexist, and anti-intellectual far too often, contributing to an indescribable amount of suffering inflicted by Christians on others. At the same time, Brian and I are among the many who have found ways to engage with Christianity that reject its temptations toward hierarchy, cruelty, and arrogance in favor of (to paraphrase Micah 6:8) justice, kindness, and humility. I have no doubt that my attempts to live out Jesus's dream, however imperfectly, have made me a better person and enabled me to contribute more to those around me. Meaning systems can work for good and ill and often work for both, depending on who is engaging with them and how.

As *meaning-making* beings, we flourish when our meaning-making is empowering for us and others, enabling all of us to live good lives and supporting our inclinations to contribute usefully to society.

We suffer when experiences of personal trauma, social chaos, or violence lead us to feel that our lives do not make sense (or that they only make sense in disempowering or fear-inducing ways). We suffer when we are not permitted to tell our story or when no one is willing to listen to our story and take it seriously (as so often happens to members of devalued groups).

Agentic Beings

We are agentic beings, which is to say that we have self-efficacy and the need to act on and have an impact on the world around us.

We may be human "beings," but we are involved in an awful lot of human doings, and those human doings contribute greatly to how we see ourselves as human beings. Undergirding most of what we do—particularly when we are doing what we want—is our human agency: our sense of purpose and the actions we take to live out that purpose.

We do not use the phrase "human agency" often, but there are many terms that point to the same attribute, including will, motivation, self-determination, initiative, capability, self-realization, and volition. We have goals, interests, and intentions, which we pursue to the extent that we have the ability. We want things and we go after what we want. We understand ourselves as having some responsibility for making our lives what we want them to be. We have the capacity to hope and plan for the future and to work for a better future for ourselves and others. Many of us would say that we want to be remembered, to make a mark on the world, to leave a legacy, to have made a difference.

Our ability to thrive depends on our capacity to control at least some aspects of our lives. We cannot choose either the religion or the economic system in which we grow up, for example; however, we can choose how to respond to them. We can stay in the religion (however comfortably or restlessly) or leave it; we can pick a career that could make us a lot of money or pick a job that lets us prioritize our family or our outside interests. It's crucial that we have the autonomy to make decisions such as these if we want to have good lives.

As *agentic* beings, we flourish when we act to pursue our goals and live out our purpose as we understand it, when we can leave a positive mark on the world and know that we have made a difference.

We suffer when we are unable to act on our desires because our autonomy is denied, safety is unavailable, or we do not have access to the resources we need to act.

Learning Beings

We are learning beings who grow and develop over the course of our lives.

We obtain information about the world from the time we are born to the time we die. Some of what we learn is gained passively by simply experiencing life through our senses. We are, however, much more than information receptacles; we also use our agency to add to our knowledge and skills. We are required to learn because there are things we have to know; we are also inspired to learn because there are things we want to know.

We learn how to get dressed, how to manage social situations, and how to accomplish mundane tasks. We learn one or more languages. We may learn how to play an instrument, a sport, or both. We learn the values, traditions, and practices of our social, religious, ancestral, or other communities. If we are disabled or have health difficulties, we learn how to navigate challenging spaces and social systems. If we belong to socially devalued groups, we learn how to survive in a society that may not care about our well-being.

We learn for work and we learn for fun. We learn in formal settings such as schools and religious venues. We learn by reading, watching TV, and surfing the web. We learn through our relationships—my father taught me how to write songs, my mother taught me how to take care of cats, and a friend taught me everything I know about analytic philosophy.

Beyond gaining knowledge and skills through training or formal study, we learn by trying things, experimenting, and exploring. I have become a better driver by taking rambling drives all over Colorado Springs, often with no particular endpoint in mind; I've also learned fascinating things about my adopted city through these drives. We may mess around with chemistry sets, baking products, or plant varieties. Because our experimenting may involve failing, we learn best when we understand failure to be a natural part of learning and when we are able to start over and try again without judgment from others after we fail at something.

While learning can require hard work, it can also provide pleasure and a sense of accomplishment. Growing intellectually, emotionally, or in other ways as a result of our learning can be rewarding whether it is growth for its own sake or growth in service to other goals. Our learning changes us beyond simply giving us new knowledge and skills. It can enable us to understand ourselves in new ways, to reinvent ourselves, to find new and greater purpose for our lives.

As *learning* beings, we flourish when we add to our knowledge, skills, and capabilities over the course of our lives, growing intellectually and personally.

We suffer when our attempts to learn are actively blocked, whether by teachers who don't believe in us or by circumstances in which we cannot access the resources and opportunities we need for learning.

Societal Beings

We are societal beings, meaning that our lives are interwoven with the larger societies of which we are a part.

Perhaps the most important insight of sociology and other social sciences is that people are not merely individuals who exist over and against "society," but that we make society and society makes us. As relational beings, we are inextricably interconnected with other individuals; as societal beings, we are inextricably interconnected with the society or societies in which we live. Specifically, we interact with, contribute to, and are affected by groups and communities, culture, organizations, and large-scale social institutions.[1]

1 Large-scale social institutions include the family, education, religion, the economy (including the marketplace), the government or state (including the military and the criminal justice system), healthcare/medicine, the media, the arts, sports, and science. In-

Our flourishing and suffering are bound up with these groups, communities, culture, organizations, and institutions. As noted earlier, our ability to flourish as learning beings depends in part on the formal educational systems with which we are involved. Our creative flourishing is enriched in societies with broad and widely available artistic opportunities. Some people's spiritual flourishing is enhanced by belonging to religious communities. On the flip side, we may be more likely to suffer physically in societies in which the government is not committed to making affordable healthcare accessible to all. These examples are only some ways in which our capacities and needs are supported (or not) by society.

As *societal* beings, we flourish when we are well-integrated into society in its many manifestations.

We suffer when we are excluded, discriminated against, or otherwise mistreated by the groups, communities, and organizations with which we interact.

Moral (and Immoral) Beings

We are moral beings, and sometimes immoral beings.

In chapter 1, I defined morally good actions as those that support human flourishing and morally problematic actions as those that contribute to otherwise avoidable suffering. Given these definitions, it's important to understand who people are as moral beings. Do we tend to carry out morally good actions? Yes, we do. Do we tend to carry out morally problematic actions? Yes, we do. Our moral complexity is a crucial part of our makeup. As so-

---

dustry and the workplace can be considered a separate institution or covered under other institutions. We generally do not interact with these institutions in the abstract but rather with the organizations that make them up: particular families, specific schools, individual religious communities, a given doctor's office, and so on.

ciologist Andrew Sayer (2011, 145) has observed, "people are ethical to the extent that they are concerned about how to act with regard to others' well-being as well as their own, precisely because they know they can easily act in ways that cause harm." Often enough, we act with regard to others' well-being; too often, we act in ways that cause harm.

If people were either entirely good or completely bad, we would never need to think about morality. If we always did the right thing or the wrong thing, ethics would not be an issue. However, for better or worse, neither the Calvinist account of utter human depravity nor the Unitarian account of inherent human goodness is fully accurate on its own. We are moral and immoral beings. As Aleksandr Solzhenitsyn (1975, 615–16) notes, "the line separating good and evil passes . . . right through every human heart." Our capacity for both morality and immorality shapes our lives and decision-making, our temptations and whether (and how) we fight them, and the state of the planet.

We love and hate. We create and destroy. We are hospitable and hostile. We can be breathtakingly generous and shockingly self-centered. We are tender to those we trust and discriminatory to those we mistrust. We urge humility and stoke fear. We mobilize for democracy and for authoritarianism. We write symphonies and craft violent manifestos. The human capacity for good is astounding; the human capacity for evil is terrifying.

We are capable of moral outrage in the face of harm; we are also capable of causing morally outrageous harm. We can work tirelessly for our own well-being and toward the well-being of others; we can also work tirelessly to promote cruelty, greed, and fear. We can comprehend concepts such as justice and fairness; how we interpret them, however, may or may not actually serve justice or fairness. Decision by decision and day by day, we can nurture our best selves or our worst selves; most of us do some of both.

As true as it is that we are morally complicated, it's also true that we have the capacity to rethink our morality and commit to living more ethically—at least as long as we have the rational capacity and the freedom to do so. In one sense, our biographies shape our future selves; in another sense, we can always start over and do better. Thus, the (accurate) description of human beings as moral and immoral does not have to be the end of the story for any of us individually or for our communities. This book would make no sense if we did not always have moral options before us.

As *moral* beings, we flourish when we live according to a moral code that makes sense to us and that leads us to treat ourselves and others well, attending to our own flourishing and to theirs.

We suffer when we cannot live according to our own best moral understanding because circumstances prevent us from making moral choices.

Creative Beings

We are creative beings, given both to making new things and to appreciating the creativity of others.

Is it really fair to say that all human beings are creative? After all, not everyone composes music, paints pictures, writes books, choreographs, or otherwise makes original artistic products. If that were the only way to understand creativity, it would not be reasonable to consider it a universal human attribute.

Fortunately, creativity is far broader than the arts. It is the process by which we make and remake ourselves and our material, cultural, and social world. We do this by generating new things, ideas, and relationships, and we engage in this process all the time.

Whenever we see something in a new way, grasp some truth about ourselves for the first time, or come up with an original joke, that's creativity. Whenever we develop new solutions for daily problems, whether that's jury-rigging a device to keep pests out of the vegetable garden, organizing the frighteningly messy pantry, or figuring out how to talk to that uncle whose politics drive us crazy, that's creativity. We improvise creatively in the kitchen by adapting a recipe while cooking, in new social situations when we're not quite sure what's going on, and in response to changes in our work schedules. Creativity is at work every time we use our energy, efforts, and insights to add something to the world that was not there before, to put existing things or ideas together in a new way, or to change something in our relationship with a friend, partner, colleague, or family member. Seen in this way, creativity is a deep and expansive part of the human experience, one in which we all partake regularly.

The organizations with which we interact are also full of creativity: workplace creativity, marketplace creativity, medical creativity, religious creativity, athletic creativity, and so on. The new product in the store, the revision to the opening prayer, and the soccer player finding an unexpected angle from which to score, all represent creativity at work and play.

Beyond our own creativity we respond to the creativity around us. Other people's creativity and their creations move us, make us think, help us learn, and invite us to live more deeply. Our own creativity is often inspired by the creativity of others whether they are people we know or whether we encounter them through their ideas or products. My own creativity has benefitted from having a songwriter father, excellent teachers and professors, and many good therapists, for example. Even if we do not see ourselves as particularly creative, however, our lives are richer for the books we read, videos we watch, music we hear, and ideas we encounter.[2]

As *creative* beings, we flourish when we are involved in the thinking of new thoughts, the making of new things, and the generating of new or deeper relationships. We flourish when we create in whatever forms have integrity for us, when our creativity is supported, and when we experience and appreciate the creativity of others.

We suffer when we are prevented from being creative and when we are denied access to the creative products or processes of other people.

Spiritual Beings

We are spiritual beings, meaning that we can experience awe, reverence, wonder, and a sense of being part of something larger than ourselves. Our spirituality can be tied to organized religion, but it does not need to be.

If it is controversial to claim that creativity is a universal human attribute, it is even more controversial to claim that spirituality is one. The term "spiritual" as commonly used simply does not describe many people who identify as secular, atheist, or humanist. As with creativity, however, I hope to describe spirituality in a way that is more convincingly universal. This section is longer than the preceding sections because spirituality requires so much care to discuss properly.

First, it is important to say something about what spirituality does not require. It is not dependent on specific doctrines or on any particular understanding of the

---

2 Of course, creativity can also be put to work in the service of cruelty, prejudice, violence, and other forms of harm. Creativity can be used for good or ill, as can all core human attributes.

sacred (for example, as an all-powerful entity or as the perfect person-writ-large). Spirituality is not dependent on our social, religious, or political identities. Atheists can have spiritual experiences, as can people within any and every faith tradition.

What, then, is spirituality? Secular sociologist Phil Zuckerman has described it this way:

> In sum, when I think of the most important, memorable, and meaningful moments of my life—moments when I feel simultaneously ephemeral and eternal, moments that define who I am and give me my deepest sense of self—I find that the title of "secular humanist" leaves a bit to be desired. I am often full of a profound, overflowing feeling. And the word that comes closest to describing that feeling is awe. So, at root, I'm an "aweist" (Zuckerman 2014, 208–9).

Zuckerman contends that the term "aweism" "encapsulates the notion that existence is ultimately a beautiful mystery, that being alive is a wellspring of wonder, and that the deepest questions of existence, creation, time, and space are so powerful as to inspire deep feelings of joy, poignancy, and sublime awe" (2014, 209). Here, Zuckerman captures both the role of feelings in spirituality and the way in which it is a response to an encounter with mystery. Similarly, writer Emily Esfahani Smith observes that "a brush with mystery—whether underneath the stars, before a gorgeous work of art, during a religious ritual, or in the hospital delivery room—can transform us" (2017, 131).

While we usually think of feelings as part of our emotional or psychological lives, spirituality involves feelings that go beyond our daily happiness, sadness, anger, and fear. Zuckerman specifically names wonder, joy, poignancy, and awe; you may have others to add.

It's not that these emotions cannot occur in our mundane lives; however, they can be understood as spiritual when they occur as a result of an encounter with what Zuckerman calls the "beautiful mystery" of existence. As Smith notes, we may encounter this mystery in many places, some defined as sacred and others thought of as secular, but all inviting us into something transcendent to which we respond with reverence and gratitude.

This transcendence can break into our lives in a multitude of ways. It might involve an encounter with the holy as we understand the holy. It may be that feeling of deep peace and calm we feel when standing on a beach alone, facing the ocean. It could be the moment during a large protest march when we feel most connected to the hundreds of justice-seekers around us. It may be the tears of joy that fall when we listen to a song that touches our spirits, offers hope, and invites us into wholeness. It could be the moment of breathlessness as we are struck by the profound beauty of a painting or by the vastness of nature. It might be the combination of humility and reassurance we experience as we participate in a worship ritual that has been practiced for thousands of years by people both like and unlike us, or as we hear the truth that we cannot yet say aloud spoken at a twelve-step meeting.

Whatever else is true about transcendent mystery, it is inevitably something larger than our own egos, agendas, and preoccupations. Whether it is a work of art, a story, a community, a religious tradition, an experience of nature, or even a life project to which we devote ourselves, this transcendence brings us to our innermost depths while also taking us outside of ourselves. It offers us new insights, makes us feel things we did not know we could feel, and transforms us. We are different after we have met the mystery—more open to surprise, more thankful for life's abundance, perhaps even more trusting.

Spirituality is not only about the experiences we have, however; it is also about the perspective and resilience that we cultivate for ourselves through spiritual practices. Patience amidst chaos, hopefulness when everything seems hopeless, and kindness in the face of cruelty are all developed through our efforts at meditation, prayer, compassionate acts, generosity, or solidarity with devalued communities. When we choose love over fear, forgiveness over vengeance, or selflessness over greed, we are strengthening our spiritual muscles. Even our ability to be present and awake for those moments of transcendence that come unbidden depends on our capacity to quiet our minds and gently set our anxiety or regret aside.

As *spiritual* beings, we flourish when we encounter the transcendent mystery in whatever form or forms it takes, and our lives are filled with gratitude, awe, wonder, humility, and reverence in response. We flourish when we know ourselves to be part of something larger than ourselves.

We suffer when we are cut off from the experiences, opportunities, and resources that can help us cultivate a mindset of openness to transcendence. We suffer when we experience the world as inherently bleak, chaotic, violent, and dangerous—worthy of fear but not of gratitude, wonder, or awe.

A Cautionary Note

It's important to acknowledge that flourishing is never guaranteed. For example, someone might live in a physically and emotionally safe environment, have access to survival resources and good healthcare, and have bodily autonomy, and still fail to live joyfully and efficaciously in their body. Nonetheless, without these preconditions, bodily well-being falls somewhere between unlikely and impossible. The same is true about other kinds of flourishing.

It's also important to acknowledge how aspirational many of these preconditions are for most people. Few societies are deeply committed to making sure that everyone in them has the opportunity for a good life, especially given the complexities of who we are as human beings. For most political leaders and other decision-makers in positions of power, supporting basic human needs for all people is not even an idea under serious consideration, let alone a priority that guides policy-making or other substantial decisions. In fact, plenty of policy-making leads to avoidable suffering for far too many people.

If we want the opportunity to have good lives and if we believe that all people should get to have good lives—joyous, fulfilling, empowered lives—we need to start with this sobering reality and determine how we might change the situation, individually and collectively.

The Intersection of Human Attributes

While I have separated out the discussion of our core human attributes to help us think about them more clearly, all ten attributes intersect with one another across our lives—another example of humanity's amazing complexity.

For example, we experience emotions, relate to other people, make sense of the world, act as agents, learn and grow, interact with society, behave morally (and immorally), create, and have spiritual experiences through our senses and through our bodies more broadly.

We find the passion and energy to create, learn, live morally, and make a difference in the world through our emotions. Moreover, our spirituality is bound up with our emotions such that when we experience expansive joy, deep gratitude, or abiding hope, we might use either psychological or religious language to describe those experiences.

Because our meaning-making shapes our decisions and actions, how we make sense of the world impacts everything from how we use our bodies and understand our emotions to how we relate to others, exercise our agency in the world, learn, and create. Our morality is dependent on our meaning-making, from what behaviors count as moral or immoral to what kinds of people we understand as moral or immoral (and why). Conversely, our meaning-making is shaped by society and its institutions (e.g., education, religion, the arts) from which we learn how to make sense of the world.

Finally (though many other examples are possible), we use our bodies, our emotions, our relationships, our agency, our meaning-making, our learning, our moral (and immoral) impulses, and even our spirituality in our creative lives.

In short, our human attributes inform, enrich, and complicate one another.[3]

---

3 How the attributes inform each other in our lives may be very different depending on our individual experiences and how we make sense of the world. Consider two hypothetical men. Both are part of a religious system that does not affirm LGBTQ+ identities. Both are also gay. One may eventually modify or jettison his religious beliefs in order to accept and live into his sexuality. We might say that he has prioritized his embodied (and perhaps his relational) flourishing and reworked his meaning-making around it. The other man might choose to live a celibate life based on the importance of his beliefs to his identity and sense of self. We might say that he has deprioritized one aspect of his embodied flourishing because of the centrality of his meaning system.

Integrated Flourishing, Aggravated Suffering

The ten attributes described in this chapter—embodiment, emotions, relationality, meaning-making, sociality, agency, learning, morality, creativity, and spirituality—do not capture the entirety of what it means to be human, but they describe important aspects of our lives. Even as our individual experiences of living with these attributes differ, their central role in our lives is undeniable.

Some attributes, such as our embodiment, exist at all times. While we are alive, we are embodied. Other attributes, such as creativity and spirituality, describe experiences we have at times and capabilities that we may or may not cultivate. But each attribute is like a thread woven into the larger tapestry of our lives. When every thread has integrity, the tapestry is stronger and more beautiful. If any thread is torn, the tapestry is weakened and diminished.

We can, therefore, define integrated flourishing as the well-being that results from flourishing across multiple human attributes. The more we flourish in the context of each attribute, and the more attributes across which we flourish, the greater our overall well-being, the richer our lives, and the more we can tend to others and contribute to society.

The same is true of avoidable suffering. We can experience avoidable suffering across multiple human attributes in ways that build on one another, making it harder for us to flourish. Aggravated suffering limits our well-being as well as our ability to give back to others.

Working to flourish and to help others flourish means aiming for integrated flourishing, well-being that cuts across our different attributes. For example, when our embodiment nourishes our spirituality, our meaning-making enriches our emotions, and our learning informs our creativity, we have access to greater joy and efficacy as well as an expanded capacity for both gratitude and service to others. Similarly, working against our own avoidable suffering and against the avoidable suffering of others means attending to the different ways that suffering can build up across these core attributes so that we can minimize the aggravated nature of that suffering.

While none of us can guarantee anyone's flourishing (including our own), all of us can work to make sure that the preconditions of flourishing are in place for us and others, and indeed for all people, and we can work against our own suffering and the suffering of others. In chapter 3, I consider the important role of systemic inequality in shaping our flourishing and suffering.

3

Flourishing, Suffering, and Inequality

Justice-making attends to how people's well-being is enhanced or diminished by prevailing patterns of social power and powerlessness . . . [In an] inclusive, participatory social order [power] is fairly distributed and used to build community, goods and resources are equitably produced and shared, and people thrive because they are deeply valued, cared for, and respected in all their diversity. (Marvin Ellison, Erotic Justice, *1996, 2)*

An ethic of flourishing has implications for our day-to-day decision-making and actions. For example, if we care about our own embodied flourishing, we need to take action to make sure that we are safe from trauma and violence, that we have access to the resources necessary for physical health, and that we are free to use our bodies for pleasure, empowerment, and accomplishment. If we care about the embodied flourishing of others, we need to take action to make sure that the same preconditions hold for them; this is true both for specific people we know and for humanity more broadly.

If we care about emotional flourishing, or meaning-making flourishing, or any other kind of flourishing, we have the same opportunity to choose values, words, and actions that support such flourishing and that minimize avoidable suffering. We can make these choices as individuals and as communities. Prioritizing flourishing can guide our personal, interactional, and political decisions once we understand flourishing in the concrete ways that I have described.

While tending to our own flourishing is important, if we care about the well-being of all people, we also will want to understand the larger systemic forces that enhance flourishing, limit it, or cause avoidable suffering. The better we understand society's role in helping people flourish or causing them to suffer, the greater a part we can play in changing society so that more people can flourish and fewer people will suffer. For example, recent research shows how the United States' political policies can impact flourishing and suffering even to the point of lengthening or shortening lives (Johnson 2022).

There are many ways to understand the connection between large-scale social and political patterns and human well-being or the lack of it. Because systemic inequality, such as white supremacy, sexism, and heterosexism, plays a substantial role in our opportunities or lack of opportunities to flourish, such inequality is worth its own consideration and is the subject of this chapter.

As wonderful as it would be to live in a world where everyone was fully committed to both their own flourishing and the flourishing of other people, that's not the world in which we live. In most societies, members of socially, politically, and economically valued groups are perfectly content to let others suffer even as they benefit from systemic inequality. Moreover, the flourishing of some people is linked directly to the suffering of others.

For example, in the U.S., white supremacy means that my whiteness grants me benefits that members of BIPOC communities rarely receive while protecting me from harms that they regularly experience. This is most frequently expressed in my receiving the benefit of the doubt from other white people as I move through my days, both in institutional contexts and in public settings. People will assume the best about me and expect the best from me when they do not have any evidence about what I am actually like. They may presume that I am competent and successful at my job or at whatever else I choose to do. They may assume that I am intelligent, trustworthy, moral, and financially stable—a positive contributor to society. They may expect me to be rational, reasonable, and harmless. People may decide that I am worthy of respect and that I deserve to be treated fairly, to receive justice, and to have my rights honored. Again, in the context of this discussion, those assumptions are being made about me because I'm white.

Receiving the benefit of the doubt from white people is important in societies in which white people have a great deal of decision-making power. When introducing the idea of societal flourishing in chapter 2, I mentioned the importance of institutions to our well-being. One of the ways institutions shape our lives is by granting some people the legitimate authority to make decisions about other people's lives that will enhance or diminish the well-being of those people. When someone has institutional decision-making power, society will often accept the decisions they make as appropriate because they are acting on behalf of the institution they represent.

Teachers, loan officers, police, politicians, judges, and corporate executives are among those with decision-making power. They have access to social, cultural, political, or economic resources that they can share, restrict, or divide up as they see fit. Moreover, they can choose to leave me alone, monitor me suspiciously, or restrict my actions. When I take a class, try to get a mortgage, drive above the speed limit, or start a new job, it is important that the people with the institutional power to treat me well or badly choose to treat me well, to give me the benefit of the doubt.

It is just as important that strangers give me the benefit of the doubt when I'm out in public so that I can get to where I'm going without being harassed or attacked. The stranger in question might not have any formal decision-making authority but still, they could choose to leave me alone or to make my life difficult. As a white person out in public among other white people, I am likely to receive the benefit of the doubt and be left alone.

In a white supremacist society, members of BIPOC communities are more likely to have the benefit of the doubt withheld from them—both by white people with decision-making power and in white public spaces. In both contexts, white people may assume the worst about BIPOC people and expect the worst from them, again without any evidence about what they are actually like as individuals.

White supremacist assumptions can lead white people to believe that members of BIPOC communities are incompetent, unsuccessful, unintelligent, untrustworthy, immoral, and financially unstable. Members of BIPOC communities may be viewed as irrational or unreasonable (thus the stereotype of the "angry Black man or woman") and are often treated (by police officers and vigilantes, for example) as dangerous. White people who make these assumptions may feel that members of BIPOC communities do not merit or deserve the same respect they would expect for themselves.

Social psychologist Susan Opotow (1990) describes this phenomenon as "moral exclusion": the processes and practices by which some people are defined as outside the "moral community" within which people are understood as deserving of moral treatment. White supremacy often involves excluding members of BIPOC communities from the (white) moral community. When members of these communities are morally excluded, white people find it morally unproblematic to treat them unfairly, to deny them justice, and to ignore their rights.

While I have used white supremacy as an example, the same processes drive sexism, heterosexism, transphobia, Islamophobia, xenophobia, ableism, ageism, and all other forms of systemic inequality. Many of us receive the benefit of the doubt in some contexts and are denied it in others. Decision-makers tend to treat me well as a white person but sometimes treat me badly as a woman or queer person. For example, while I have never been harassed or attacked on the street as a white person, I have been as a woman and as a queer person.

Given this way of thinking about inequality, let's consider some preconditions of flourishing. Broadly speaking, there are four preconditions without which flourishing will be more difficult if not impossible, and without which avoidable suffering is more likely.

The first type of flourishing precondition is access to resources, experiences, and opportunities that support flourishing. These can be survival resources for our bodies and meaning-making resources (such as information) that help us make sense of the world. They can be physical and mental health resources that people will use to different degrees but to which everyone needs access. They can be resources to help us learn, make moral choices, create new ideas or things, or grow spiritually. Similarly, we need access to experiences and opportunities that will enrich our lives, help us develop, and help us enrich the lives of others. While the list of specific experiences and opportunities that fall into these categories is long and would vary from person to person, such experiences and opportunities clearly contribute to our well-being.

The second type of flourishing precondition is safety: freedom from harm, trauma, mistreatment, violence, and danger. Physical, sexual, and emotional harm come to mind first, but we may be harmed in other ways as well. We are harmed as meaning-makers when we are unable to make sense of our experiences. We are harmed morally when we are forced to behave in ways that go against our moral sensibility as the growing literature on "moral injury" suggests (Norman and Maguen, n.d.). Safety, as described here, includes freedom from fear, since fear of potential harm can itself be psychologically and physically damaging over time.

The third type of flourishing precondition is autonomy and self-determination, or what we more commonly call freedom or independence. We need physical autonomy as "body-selves" (Nelson 1978, 20); we also need other kinds of self-determination to flourish emotionally, relationally, as meaning-makers and story-tellers, as learners and teachers, and as creators. We cannot live truly moral lives without the freedom to make and act on moral decisions and we cannot live spiritual lives without the freedom to cultivate our spirituality in whatever way makes sense for us. Most basically, we cannot act as agents in the world without some degree of independence.

The fourth type of flourishing precondition is in a sense the reverse of the second type: respect and positive treatment by other individuals and by the communities and organizations with which we interact. At the most personal level this involves experiencing love and belonging from the people we care about the most. More broadly it means being welcome in any social context in which we find ourselves.

We can also think about respect and positive treatment as moral inclusion. If moral exclusion, as described earlier, involves defining some people as outside the moral community and as, therefore, undeserving of moral treatment, we need moral inclusion to flourish. We need to be part of the community of people seen as deserving of moral treatment. In our interactions with strangers, both in public places and in organizational contexts, this means that we need to receive the benefit of the doubt. We need people to presume that we are (for example) trustworthy, dependable, competent, moral, and harmless, and to treat us accordingly.

If we consider the concrete ways in which systemic inequality plays out, we'll notice that members of devalued groups cannot count on having these preconditions available to them. They cannot count on having access to the resources, experiences, and opportunities that support flourishing. They cannot count on safety or freedom from harm, trauma, mistreatment, violence, and danger. They cannot count on having their autonomy and self-determination respected by others, whether those others are individuals or social institutions. And they cannot count on respect and positive treatment across society. In contrast, members of valued groups can often count on all of these preconditions. Those of us who belong both to valued and devalued groups can count on these preconditions in some contexts but not others. Let's take sexism and anti-Black racism as examples.[1]

In sexist societies, women make less money than men, must fear rape and sexual assault in ways that most men

---

1 Because of how brief this discussion is, I do not address intersectionality, the process by which (for example) Black women experience the worst aspects of both sexism and anti-Black racism (including specific ways in which Black women, but not white women or Black men, are denied the benefit of the doubt).

need not, have less control over what they do with their bodies (both legally and in terms of cultural expectations), and face various types of disrespect and negative treatment ranging from street harassment to hiring discrimination. Society doubts (female) accusers and protects (male) abusers. Women are assumed to be less competent as political leaders. Many religious traditions do not allow women to be official spiritual leaders.[2]

The intellectual, cultural, artistic, and moral creativity of men has long been far more highly valued than that of women, such that men have been encouraged in ways that women have not been, though this situation is changing. Men have been provided with access to the resources, experiences, and opportunities that allowed them to develop their ideas and create their work, while women have had far less access to those resources, opportunities, and experiences. Men have been encouraged to use their bodies in a range of ways not accessible to women; sports, for example, has been a male domain for most of its history. As a result, in what sociologists would call a self-fulfilling prophecy (Merton 1948), men's success has been taken as evidence of their greater capabilities while pundits have asked why there were no great women artists (Nochlin 2015), astronomers, athletes, or anthropologists. It is still more common to consider men brilliant and to expect great things of them (Gajewski 2020). These are just some of the concrete ways in which society supports the flourishing of men more than the flourishing of women.

Anti-Black racism in the United States began before the country came into being. Slavery denied the full humanity

2 National Partnership for Women & Families n.d.; Kuadli 2022; New Jersey Coalition against Sexual Assault 2022; Hesse 2022; Valenti 2008; University of California San Diego Center on Gender Equity and Health/Stop Street Harassment 2019; Quadlin 2018; Tuerkheimer 2021; Bauer 2020; "Ordination of Women" n.d.

and self-determination of African Americans. Later, the federal government and white citizens colluded in segregating neighborhoods, preventing African Americans from building up housing equity and thereby wealth, while also condemning them to inadequate, under-resourced schools. Police officers and vigilantes target and kill African Americans disproportionately. Racial discrimination has been documented across the criminal justice system, in housing markets, in education, in hiring, in healthcare provision, and in other institutions as well as in public venues such as stores. While anti-Black racism is far more extensive than this description suggests, the discrimination mentioned here demonstrates the range of ways in which white US Americans fail to give African Americans the benefit of the doubt or treat them with respect.[3]

While I will never know the pain, fear, and exhaustion that comes with facing anti-Black racism, my experiences as a woman and queer person have given me insight into the emotional, mental, and physical challenges of living in a discriminatory society. Years of street harassment have been embarrassing and sometimes terrifying. I still recall the stress of waiting to hear whether the Supreme Court would allow my same-sex marriage to remain legal. I also remember the tension of walking into a bakery to order a wedding cake, unsure of whether the bakery would be willing to make it for us or not.

The grief and fear I experienced following the mass shooting at Club Q described in the introduction was exacerbated by my rage at finding out that more than 300 state bills were introduced to limit LGBTQ+ student and teacher rights across the United States in 2022 alone (Hamilton 2022). Over time, the emotions that these kinds

3 Rothstein 2017; Garcia 2020; Balko 2020; Faber 2018; Korver-Glenn 2021; Losen and Martinez 2020; Kline, Rose and Walters 2021; Villarosa 2022; Singletary 2018.

of situations bring up can take a mental and physical toll.[4] While I have a rich and wonderful life for which I am grateful, it has been harder than it would have been in a society without sexism and heterosexism. The same could be said by any member of a devalued group about the inequality that limits their flourishing or causes avoidable suffering.

Systemic inequality interferes with flourishing and contributes to avoidable suffering even beyond its impact on members of devalued groups. When people cannot flourish or when they experience avoidable suffering due to inequality, the rest of the world is robbed of the contributions they might otherwise offer. African American author Ralph Ellison (2014) wrote, "this is a world in which the major energy of the [Black] imagination goes not into creating works of art but into overcoming the frustrations of social discrimination." What a tragedy, and what a waste of brilliance and creativity.

Of course, systemic inequality does not merely damage flourishing or cause avoidable suffering; it also ends lives prematurely. When I consider the BIPOC lives lost to poverty and to police and vigilante violence, the LGBTQ+ lives lost to antigay and anti-trans violence and to suicide, and the lives of women lost to domestic violence, I mourn—for those individuals and their families, certainly, but also for the rest of us. We have lost their energy, wisdom, insights and hope. We have lost their beauty and kindness, their friendship and their efforts to make the world a more loving place. This loss is incalculable.

---

4 Examples of the extensive literature on physical and mental impacts of racism, sexism, and heterosexism include Bailey et al 2017; Cornell University Public Policy Research Portal 2019; Geronimus 2023; Goosby, Cheadle and Mitchell 2018; Harnois and Bastos 2018; Mahowald, Gruberg and Halpin 2020; Rooney n.d.; Sima 2023; Simons et al 2018; Trevor Project 2022.

Systemic inequality is, simply, antithetical to the flourishing of all people. It limits flourishing and causes avoidable suffering, especially for members of devalued groups but secondarily for others as well. A moral commitment to the flourishing of all people, therefore, necessarily invites us to work against systemic inequality in all its forms—both individually and as part of larger movements for change.

Sometimes this invitation means working for the well-being of groups to which we do not belong. If I benefit from being white in a white supremacist society, and if those benefits help me flourish, that means members of BIPOC communities in my society are being penalized for their race and are suffering needlessly. If I care about their flourishing, I must join in the struggle against white supremacy—which is also a struggle to increase joy and decrease pain for members of BIPOC communities.

At the same time, we are invited to work for the well-being of groups to which we belong so that we ourselves may flourish more and suffer less. If I care about my own well-being and the well-being of other women and LGBTQ+ people, I will naturally want to be part of the struggles against sexism and heterosexism—which are also struggles to increase joy and decrease pain for these communities to which I belong.

In part 1, we've explored what it might look like to base our ethics on the well-being of actual people rather than on abstract principles and values. I've made claims about flourishing and avoidable suffering, described important aspects of our common humanity, listed specific preconditions that can set us up for the potential to have good lives, and noted situations under which we might suffer unnecessarily. Finally, I've considered how systemic inequality makes integrated flourishing impossible for members of devalued groups, ultimately harming all of us, and have invited us to begin (or continue) to work against systemic inequality for the sake of expanding human joy and decreasing human pain.

While this ethical approach might be valuable to people in various religious traditions and outside religion entirely, I believe it will resonate particularly well with progressive Christians. Jesus invited people to participate in the making of God's kin-dom. One way to follow Jesus today is to strive to bring the kin-dom into being as a community of flourishing. In part 2, I examine how both the biblical tradition (chapter 4) and contemporary progressive Christian thought (chapter 5) are compatible with an ethic of flourishing. I then offer ideas about what we might do individually and communally to build up societies of well-being in line with Jesus's proclamation and invitation.

Part 2:
The Kin-dom of God as a Community of Flourishing

4

Jesus, the Prophets, and Beyond

I think about the life of Jesus and how it seems that every time Jesus has the chance to put rules, regulations, interpretations, or anything else above his relationship with a person, he always chooses the person. When put to task about what the "greatest commandment" is, he points toward two relationships: the love between God and people, and the love between two people. (Brian Hehn, 2019 email from the Hymn Society in the US and Canada)

In Mark's Gospel, Jesus's ministry begins with the words, "The time is fulfilled, and the [kin-dom] of God has come near; repent, and believe in the good news" (Mark 1:15).[1] In Matthew's Gospel, Jesus teaches his disciples to pray for God's kin-dom to come and for God's will to be done on earth (Matthew 6:10). For Jesus, God's kin-dom, God's

1 Biblical quotations are from the New Revised Standard Version. I have made a few minor modifications. In cases where Matthew or Luke use material that appears in Mark, I use the Marcan version in keeping with biblical scholarship indicating that Mark's Gospel was written before Matthew or Luke wrote their Gospels.

will, and the good news are tied up in one another. Jesus never uses the term "flourishing" to our knowledge, but his vision of the kin-dom of God involves human well-being and the good news he proclaims is of an inbreaking realm or domain in which people can flourish—meaning that human flourishing is God's will.[2]

In this chapter, I consider passages from the synoptic Gospels (Matthew, Mark, and Luke) that support this claim, continue with examples of materials that suggest the importance of flourishing as an ethical priority from the prophetic tradition from which Jesus emerged, and conclude with two passages indicating that human well-being was a concern among the early Christian communities that developed after Jesus's death.[3] Ultimately, I agree with situation ethicist Joseph Fletcher (1966, 64) that "the New Testament calls upon us to love people, not principles."

One of those early Christian communities provided us with the Gospel according to John and its claim that Jesus "came that they may have life and have it abundantly" (John 10:10). While the abundance spoken of in that claim is spiritual and does not address the range of human attributes that I have discussed, the words and actions

---

2 Writer Derek Penwell similarly claims that, "in announcing a different kind of reign, Jesus held up a vision of the world as God intended, one in which all people flourish" (2018, 38). The worship collective Enfleshed (n.d.) has created a version of the prayer Jesus taught his disciples that translates the term "kingdom" as "holy vision for collective flourishing."

3 This chapter is exploratory rather than comprehensive, meant only to suggest the possibility of engaging with the Bible from an ethic-of-flourishing perspective. Also, in keeping with the best of contemporary biblical scholarship, I acknowledge that the authors of the Gospels were making theological claims, not providing journalistic accounts of the life of Jesus, meaning that some of what Jesus is reported to say in the Gospels was added by the Gospel writers for their own purposes.

attributed to Jesus that are most likely to be authentic suggest that Jesus was indeed invested in abundance—not just abundant life but abundant *lives*, lives characterized by flourishing.

"The Sabbath Was Made for Humankind"

Jesus disagrees with some of his community's religious leaders[4] about what is and what is not permissible to do on the sabbath, the day of rest during which Jewish law forbids work (broadly defined). When the Pharisees criticize Jesus for allowing his disciples to pick grain on the sabbath, he responds, "The sabbath was made for humankind, and not humankind for the sabbath" (Mark 2:27). This exchange is followed almost immediately by one in which Jesus asks the Pharisees, "Is it lawful to do good or to do harm on the sabbath, to save life or to kill?" when they judge him for his willingness to heal a man's withered hand on the day of rest (Mark 3:4).

Luke (13:10–17) offers a similar story in which Jesus heals a crippled woman on the sabbath and the leader of the synagogue criticizes Jesus, saying, "There are six days on which work ought to be done; come on those days and be cured, and not on the sabbath day" (Luke 13:14). Jesus responds by pointing out that observant Jews untie their animals and lead them to water to drink on the sabbath and then asks whether the woman should not be set free from her eighteen years of bondage on just such a day (Luke 13:15–16).

---

4 We must remember that Jesus was a pious and observant Jew and that there were diverse approaches to Judaism in his day. The fact that the Gospel writers choose to highlight Jesus's conflict with Jewish leadership should not lead us to think of Jesus as personally opposed to Judaism or to "the Jews" (as John's Gospel refers to them).

The idea that the sabbath was made for humankind rather than the reverse is a kind of precursor to the idea that the point or goal of principles is human flourishing. The sabbath, we might even say, was made for human well-being. Moreover, in the two stories of Jesus healing on the sabbath, he defends himself by recasting the sabbath as an opportunity to do good, save life, and liberate people from bondage rather than as a restricted period in which work is forbidden regardless of the nature or value of the work.

Love God, Your Neighbor, Yourself, and Your Enemy

When a scribe asks Jesus which commandment is the most important, Jesus responds with not one, but two commandments (Mark 12:28–34). The first is taken, slightly modified, from Deuteronomy 6:4–5: to love God with all of one's being. The second commandment is taken from Leviticus 19:18: to love one's neighbor as oneself.[5] The scribe agrees that these two commandments are "much more important than all whole burnt-offerings and sacrifices." Jesus replies that he is "not far from the [kin-dom] of God" (Mark 12:33–34).

We have encountered this passage so often that we may have become inattentive to just how radical it is. Of the hundreds of commandments Jesus could have picked, he does not choose one about food restrictions, cleanliness, sexual practices, how to worship, or how to respond to someone who has caused harm. He does not choose any of the ten commandments (Exodus 20:2–17; Deuteronomy 5:6–21). Jesus puts love first—love of God and love of humanity.

---

5 The apostle Paul and the author of the Letter of James agreed about the importance of loving one's neighbor as oneself (Romans 13:8–10; James 2:8), despite their other disagreements.

Moreover, Jesus does not need to mention the second commandment at all. The scribe asks only about the most important commandment. Jesus could answer to the scribe's satisfaction with the commandment to love God. That Jesus feels it necessary to include love of humanity is telling. That Jesus apparently thinks of that second commandment as parallel in some sense to the first commandment ("like it") is also telling. For Jesus, love of God and love of humanity are bound up with one another.

Finally, the scribe says something that Jesus finds to be so wise, true, and pious that he takes it as evidence that the scribe is "not far from the [kin-dom] of God." What does the scribe say? First, he agrees with Jesus about the importance of the commandments to love God and neighbor. Perhaps that answer alone might have sufficed to draw praise from Jesus, but the scribe continues, adding that these commandments are more important than worshipping God correctly as instructed in the Torah (the first five books of the Jewish testament). Jesus says nothing about worship practices in this exchange. He does not bring up burnt-offerings or sacrifices. The scribe makes that connection on his own, and his prioritizing love over ritual appears to impress Jesus.[6]

Beyond our obligations to love God, our neighbors, and (presumably) ourselves, Jesus invites us to love our enemies. The Sermon on the Mount includes a series of extensions in which Jesus begins, "You have heard that it was said..." and continues, "But I say to you...". In the last of these extensions (Matthew 5:43), Jesus indicates

---

6 In a sense, the apostle Paul updates this perspective in 1 Corinthians 13:1–3 when he observes that speaking in tongues, having prophetic powers, understanding mysteries, having enough faith to move mountains, giving away one's possessions, and risking martyrdom mean nothing without love.

that those listening to him have probably learned that they should hate their enemies.[7] Jesus responds to this expectation by reversing it, encouraging people to love their enemies and pray for their persecutors (Matthew 5:44). Moreover, Jesus goes on to indicate that people should do this because God cares for evil people as well as good ones, the unrighteous as well as the righteous. For Jesus, loving enemies is a way of acting as God acts. Luke's version of this material (Luke 6:27–28) extends Matthew's language: Jesus asks people to love their enemies, to do good to those who hate them, to bless those who curse them, and to pray for those who abuse them.

Jesus's two great commandments are not about principles, but about our obligation to love. If the greatest commandment is to love the holy, and if the commandment that follows from it is to love our neighbors as ourselves (which I take to include loving ourselves), and if the commandment to love is extended by Jesus even to our enemies, what does that say about Jesus's values and vision? It says that love is at the heart of Jesus's understanding. It's not that principles and religious practices are unimportant. It's that we follow those principles and observe those religious practices in the service of love. I consider the connection between love and flourishing directly in chapter 5.

---

7 The full verse includes both loving neighbor and hating enemy. We have already encountered the commandment to love one's neighbor as oneself (Leviticus 19:18). There are no biblical commandments to hate enemies, and Jesus's language ("You have heard that it was said") suggests his familiarity (and his expectation of the crowd's familiarity) with oral interpretations of Torah that encourage hatred of enemies.

The Golden Rule

We find the Golden Rule in multiple religious traditions. Matthew (7:12) and Luke (6:31) indicate that Jesus taught it as well. In Matthew's version, Jesus indicates that doing to others as you would have them do to you "is the law and the prophets," locating it at the heart of the Jewish tradition. Ethicists Christopher Panza and Adam Potthast (2010, 188) point out that the idea of loving your neighbor as yourself is also a version of the Golden Rule.

As powerful and intuitive as the Golden Rule is on its own, it is strengthened if we interpret it in terms of human flourishing. Just as I would want to be treated in ways that will enable me to flourish across the attributes discussed in chapter 2, I should similarly treat others in ways that will enable them to flourish across those same attributes. Panza and Potthast (2010, 197) note that the Golden Rule is least likely to be misused when it is layered over a compelling theory of morality. Arguably, an ethic of flourishing is the kind of theory of morality that enables us to interpret the Golden Rule productively.

The Judgment of the Nations

In Matthew's provocative parable about the Son of Man coming in glory (Matthew 25:31–46), Jesus warns his followers that the nations will ultimately be judged based on how well they took care of those in need—not on whether they believed the right things or worshipped correctly but on whether they fed the hungry, provided the thirsty with something to drink, welcomed the stranger, clothed the naked, cared for the sick, and visited the prisoner. In the parable, Jesus identifies himself with the hungry, the thirsty, the stranger, the naked, the sick, and the prisoner; tending to these people constitutes tending to Jesus, while failing them constitutes failing Jesus.

While the parable does not use the term "flourishing," it suggests that the test of whether a nation (not an individual, interestingly) has done right by Jesus is whether it supports the flourishing of those least able to thrive within its borders. The parable considers embodied flourishing (addressing hunger, thirst, nakedness and sickness), societal flourishing (welcoming the stranger), and relational flourishing (visiting the prisoner).

Jesus's Broader Ministry

Jesus does not merely offer sayings and parables in support of flourishing. His commitment to healing people, feeding them, teaching them, and keeping an open table that breaks down status hierarchies shows a deep concern with human well-being.

Moreover, Jesus is able to engage with people as individuals while recognizing both their social locations and their common humanity. In this sense, Jesus has a complex understanding of who the people around him are and what they need. In his words and his actions, Jesus indicates that it is God's will that people should have access to abundant lives and should be treated in ways that free them from avoidable suffering.

From Jesus to the Prophets

Jesus's valuing of people and commitment to their well-being follows in the prophetic Jewish tradition from which he emerged. This tradition stresses justice, compassionate treatment of the poor, peacemaking, and taking care of the orphan, widow, and other disempowered people. Such prophetic values are in keeping with a moral commitment to enabling all people to have good lives. But we can go further and say that Jesus sees himself as a modern-day prophet, bringing flourishing to those in pain and struggle. Consider the first time Jesus proclaims his message and ministry according to Luke:

> When he came to Nazareth . . . he went to the synagogue on the sabbath . . . He stood up to read, and the scroll of the prophet Isaiah was given to him. He unrolled the scroll and found the place where it was written: "The Spirit of the Lord is upon me, because he has anointed me to bring good news to the poor. He has sent me to proclaim release to the captives . . . to let the oppressed go free, to proclaim the year of the Lord's favor." . . . Then he began to say to them, "Today this scripture has been fulfilled in your hearing." (Luke 4:16–19, 21)

The passage on which Jesus is most likely drawing (Isaiah 62:1–2) is based on a vision of Israel's return from exile hundreds of years earlier and was never intended by whoever wrote it as a prediction of the future. Jesus, however, understands it as a blueprint for a program of liberation, wellness, and wholeness that he himself is beginning to undertake.

For what, then, did those earlier prophets yearn? What kind of world did they envision? Certainly, they sought a world of peace in which peace was a precondition of flourishing. Isaiah (2:4) and Micah (4:3) use the same language to describe such a world: "They shall beat their swords into ploughshares, and their spears into pruning-hooks; nation shall not lift up sword against nation, neither shall they learn war anymore."[8] Micah extends

---

8 Isaiah and Micah were contemporaries who prophesied in Judah, the southern kingdom of what is now Israel. Perhaps they were familiar with each other's work, or perhaps both had access to the same source material that provided this common language.

the vision further, dreaming that "they shall all sit under their own vines and under their own fig trees, and no one shall make them afraid" (Micah 4:4).

When Jesus praises the scribe for recognizing that love is more important than religious rituals (Mark 12:33–34), he recalls another prophetic insight from Micah (6:8): "[God] has told you, O mortal, what is good; and what does the holy require of you but to do justice, and to love kindness, and to journey humbly with your God?"

This beautiful verse is Micah's response to a passage (6:6–7) in which the prophet imagines Israel's questions about how to regain God's favor after failing its end of the covenant with God: "With what shall I come before the Lord and bow myself before God on high? Shall I come before God with burnt-offerings, with calves a year old? Will the Lord be pleased with thousands of rams, with tens of thousands of rivers of oil? Shall I give my firstborn for my transgression, the fruit of my body for the sin of my soul?"

With these questions, which I find to have an air of panic about them, Micah envisions what Israel thinks it needs to do for redemption: worship and sacrifice correctly in order to win God over again. In the context of the questions and the assumptions behind them, Micah's response is extraordinary: God does not require endless sacrifices, only love of people in its social form (justice), love of people in its interpersonal form (kindness), and love of God (a life of humility). By engaging in these forms of love, Israel will honor its covenant with God and will have the opportunity to flourish as a community and as individuals.

Did Jesus understand Micah 6:8 in this way? It is impossible to know, but the parallel between Micah 6:6–8 and Mark 12:28–34 is powerful. Love is "much more important than all whole burnt-offerings and sacrifices" (Mark 12:33) and understanding this brings one close to the kin-dom of God, the holy realm of flourishing.

The prophetic concern with human well-being is also particularly clear in the frequency with which the prophets remind Israel about its need to care for widows, orphans, and aliens (or strangers) in the land—and thus, to tend to the well-being of the poorest and those most at risk of suffering in the community. This reminder includes a second reminder: that Israel's obligation to care for the least of these is tied to its own story of how God cared for the Israelites when they were oppressed. The prophets draw on passages from the Torah to offer these reminders. In the Torah, the Israelites are instructed to treat aliens (or strangers) well and to love them as God loves them (Deuteronomy 10:18), for they have been aliens (or strangers) in another land (Exodus 23:9, Leviticus 19:34, Deuteronomy 10:19). Aliens are subject to the same laws as the Israelites (Numbers 15:16). The Torah provides specific guidance for making sure the poor and the stranger have access to food at harvest time (Leviticus 23:22, Deuteronomy 14:28–29). God's desire is for justice for the alien, orphan, and widow (Deuteronomy 10:18, 24:17), and the same commandments that protect the well-being of strangers protect the well-being of widows and orphans (Deuteronomy 14:28–29).

Perhaps unsurprisingly then, the prophets share a foundational concern for the poorest and least well-protected (Isaiah 1:17, Zechariah 7:8–10). Isaiah (1:23) castigates powerful people who do not take care of the orphan and widow, and who in fact harm them, a criticism echoed by Jesus hundreds of years later (Mark 12:40).

Early Christian Communities

Much of the earliest information we have about the first Christian communities comes from the authentic letters of Paul, who does not focus on the kinds of proto-flourishing values I have discussed above. However, there are two telling passages in the New Testament suggesting that human well-being was important for at least some of these communities.

One of these passages comes from the Acts of the Apostles (4:32, 34–35), written by the same author(s) as the Gospel according to Luke. The passage describes the community as follows:

> Now the whole group of those who believed were of one heart and soul, and no one claimed private ownership of any possessions, but everything they owned was held in common . . . There was not a needy person among them, for as many as owned lands or houses sold them and brought the proceeds of what was sold. They laid it at the apostles' feet, and it was distributed to each as any had need.

Clearly, this passage describes a community invested in the flourishing of all of its members—so much so that the wealthy voluntarily give up their wealth so that the least wealthy have survival resources.

Another passage that highlights the importance of tending to the poorest in the community comes from James (2:15–18): "If a sibling is naked and lacks daily food, and one of you says to them, 'Go in peace; keep warm and eat your fill,' and yet you do not supply their bodily needs, what is the good of that? So, faith by itself, if it has no works, is dead . . . Show me your faith without works, and I by my works will show you my faith."

There are two intriguing components of this text. The first component is the concrete situation described, in which kind words of support are not sufficient to address actual survival needs. James does not object to the kind words of support but finds them useless unless they are accompanied by actions that provide the survival resources necessary for the community member. At least as interesting is the broader lesson James draws from the concrete example: faith requires works or it is not meaningful. People can believe what they will and say what they like but if they are not tending to the flourishing of those around them, their faith is "dead."[9]

Ultimately, whether it is Jesus valuing love over rules and rituals, the prophets assuring Israel that God wants caring relationships rather than extravagant sacrifices, or the early Christian communities lifting up the well-being of the poorest among them, the Bible suggests that human flourishing was important to our ancestors and their ancestors. It can be important for us, their descendants, as well. In chapter 5, I explore how some contemporary progressive Christians bring together understandings of God and love with a commitment to human well-being and suggest how we might embody Jesus's invitation to love.

---

9 Several New Testament authors use the term "good works" in ways similar to James's use of "works" here (Matthew 5:16, Ephesians 2:10, Titus 3:8 and 3:14, 1 Timothy 5:25 and 6:18, 2 Thessalonians 2:17).

5

Love, Flourishing, and God

[L]ove is giving oneself to nurture another's full humanity, concerned with [their] healing, wholeness, growth, and transformation. (Kurt Struckmeyer, An Unorthodox Faith, *2017, 171)*

To love is to act intentionally, in relational response to God and others, to promote overall well-being. (Thomas Oord, Pluriform Love, *2022, 28)*

In the synoptic Gospels, Jesus names love as the central requirement for living a holy life. He also supports (and in some cases demands) actions that tend lovingly to those most at risk of suffering. In prioritizing love as a value and in inviting his followers to prioritize actions built on that value, Jesus follows in the path of the prophets and inspires early Christian communities.

If we seek to follow Jesus today or even to simply live into his vision of God's kin-dom, we need to give love pride of place, both as a value and as a guide to action. What, however, does that mean practically? How are we to go about building our lives around love, both as individuals and as communities? Since Jesus invites us to love God, our neighbors, ourselves, and our enemies, how exactly should we do that? Moreover, since Jesus, his ancestors, and his followers seem to have thought that love had something to do with human well-being, how might we connect love more concretely to the ethic of flourishing I described in part 1 of this book? In this chapter, I develop answers to these questions.

We need to begin with a new definition of love. Psychiatrist Scott Peck (1978, 81) famously defined love as "the will to extend one's self for the purposes of nurturing one's own or another's spiritual growth." This definition is helpful in moving beyond describing love as a feeling and is even more helpful in discerning the ways in which love has something to do with human flourishing, but it comes with its own limitations. First, Peck defines love as the *will* to extend ourselves but does not say anything about the actual *work* we must do to "extend" ourselves for our own well-being or for the well-being of others. We need a definition of love that includes both the desire for human well-being and the actions we take based on that desire. Second, Peck's definition focuses on immediate relationships rather than on society as a whole. We need a definition of love that includes our own flourishing and the flourishing of those we know personally while also incorporating the flourishing of our neighbors (broadly defined, per Luke 10:25–37) and our enemies. Finally, Peck's definition focuses on "spiritual growth." While spiritual flourishing is important, it is only part of a life of integrated well-being. We need a definition of love that addresses flourishing across the range of human attributes described in part 1 of this book.

My definition of love expands on Peck's version. I define love as *the work we do to flourish in all aspects of our lives and to help all other people flourish in all aspects of their lives*. Peck's "will to extend ourselves" is included here, but is subsumed under our actual efforts. His mention of self and personally known others is also included but, again, is subsumed under a broad commitment to the well-being of all humanity. Peck's mention of spiritual growth is similarly included but is subsumed under the larger list of human attributes through which we flourish.

Self-love becomes a way of understanding our commitment to our own well-being, including the actions we take to flourish. Our love of particular others becomes a way of understanding our commitment to their well-being, including the actions we take to support their flourishing. Our love of humanity is demonstrated in the work we do to help all people to flourish.

At this point, it's worth pausing and remembering how concrete human well-being is to Jesus, the prophets, and the earliest Christian communities. Love involves feeding the hungry, giving the thirsty something to drink, clothing the naked, welcoming the stranger, caring for the sick, and visiting the prisoner. Love involves being sure that poor people and aliens (or strangers) have access to food at harvest time. Love involves providing for the bodily needs of those who are hungry and insufficiently protected from the elements. For the wealthy, love involves selling their possessions and offering the money to their community so that everyone in the community has survival resources. Love involves a lot more than believing the right things, feeling the right things, saying the right things, or carrying out the right rituals.

We can better appreciate the specificity of love's demands on us today by considering some preconditions of flourishing. I use embodied flourishing as an example, though any of the ten human attributes covered would be fair to consider.

Loving ourselves and others means:

- ensuring that we and they have access to resources necessary for survival (clothes, shelter, nutritious and safe food, clean water, clean air, and sanitary environments);
- ensuring that we and they have access to appropriate, comprehensive, and affordable healthcare;
- protecting our safety and the safety of others, keeping ourselves and others free from physical and sexual violence and other kinds of harm;
- protecting ourselves and others from emotional stressors such as trauma and protracted fear that can wear on bodies over time; and
- ensuring bodily autonomy for ourselves and for others so that all of us have control over how we use our bodies and over what happens to our bodies.

If we love ourselves, we will do what we can to be sure that embodied flourishing (and the other kinds of flourishing) are real possibilities for us and we will strive to live the richest, fullest, most joyful lives we can. If we love other people, we will do what we can to be sure that embodied flourishing (and the other kinds of flourishing) are real possibilities for them so that they are free and able to strive to live the richest, fullest, and most joyful lives they can.

Some concrete examples might be helpful here. My spouse broke her left arm badly while I was writing this book and needed help with mundane tasks like dressing and cleaning herself for several weeks. During this period, I dressed and undressed her daily, cleaned parts of her body that she could not reach, and changed her bandages, striving to cause as little pain as possible while negotiating splint straps and a sling. These tasks, which could be difficult and time-consuming, were acts of love and service. I often found myself thinking about Jesus washing his disciples' feet as I put sleeping socks on my spouse at night, took them off in the morning, and put on her sandals for the day.

The care and support of family and friends was invaluable during this difficult period. They brought food, shared in the responsibilities of driving my spouse around, and made themselves available when I needed to talk. Their visits distracted her and gave me breaks, making the time a little easier for both of us. I remain grateful for their many acts of love.

Helping others flourish is not always pure labor, of course. I often feel deep joy while accompanying hymns at church, helping college students carry out ethical research at my job, or giving my dog the medicine which I know makes him feel better. Ultimately, both the hard work and the delightful work is part of the making of a world of flourishing.

Acting in love in these ways is not always easy but it offers us a way to order our lives, set priorities, and balance our own well-being with the well-being of others—again, both those we know and those we will never meet. It offers us a way to co-create the kin-dom of God in our time.

God as Love

Love as a commitment to human flourishing does not require any particular understanding of God, or even a belief in God. Where, then, does God come into the picture for those approaching an ethic of flourishing from a progressive Christian perspective? What does loving God with all our being look like in the context of this approach to ethics? We might start with some passages from the First Letter of John:

> But anyone who does not love does not know God, for God is love. (1 John 4:8)
>
> So we have known and believe the love that God has for us. God is love, and those who abide in love abide in God, and God abides in them. (1 John 4:16)
>
> No one has ever seen God; if we love one another, God lives in us, and God's love is perfected in us. (1 John 4:12)
>
> Those who say, "I love God," and hate their siblings, are liars; for those who do not love a sibling whom they have seen, cannot love God whom they have not seen. The commandment we have from God is this: those who love God must love their siblings also. (1 John 4:20–21)

Progressive Christian theologian Kurt Struckmeyer (2016, 62; italics in the original) observes of these passages:

> When the Bible declares that God is love, it means that these two language symbols—*God* and *love*—are identical. If God is love, then the converse is also true: Love is god. Therefore, the word *God* is a name we give to the spirit of selfless love found at the depths of our humanity and experienced in the relationship of human love toward one another . . . When we say that God is love . . . God becomes an immanent reality within our hearts, within our minds, within our relationships, and in our actions.

Struckmeyer is not alone among contemporary progressive Christians in identifying God with love and in understanding love lived out in service of human well-being as holy. Progressive Christian pastor and author Phillip Gulley (2018, 193–194) has similarly commented, "I believe God is that essence in us that reaches out to another, committed to their well-being, their enlightenment, their moral, emotional, relational, and spiritual growth."

Following Struckmeyer and Gulley, we might add to the many ways people understand God by proposing that *God is incarnated and made manifest as love in the work we do and the relationships we build in support of our own flourishing and the flourishing of others*. If "God is love" and love partakes of the holy, then the work we do for our own flourishing and for the flourishing of others is holy work. If avoidable suffering is, in a sense, the opposite of flourishing, then the work we do to mitigate our own avoidable suffering and the avoidable suffering of others is also holy work.

At this point, we are finally in a position to provide at least preliminary answers to the questions of how to love God, ourselves, our neighbors, and our enemies.

We can love God with all our being by striving to enable God's creation to flourish. God's creation includes all human beings—ourselves, our neighbors, our enemies, people we know, people we do not know, people we like, people we hate, people who like us, people who hate us. Jesus tells us that God makes the sun rise on both evil people and good people; God offers both the righteous and the unrighteous the nourishment of rain (Matthew 5:45). Similarly, we should desire and work for the well-being of people without regard for their moral goodness.[1]

1 I do not believe that working for the well-being of all people, including our enemies, requires us to prioritize their well-being over our own. This point is particularly true in cases where our

Loving God with all our being also means striving to enable the natural world and its non-human creatures to flourish. Humans cannot ultimately flourish when the planet is suffering, particularly given the extent to which humans are responsible for planetary suffering. Human well-being is not, however, the only reason to become better stewards of the planet and of non-human lives; it is not even the most important reason. If we understand sacred love as infusing all creation, we must cultivate our own love toward non-human creation, which in turn means supporting its well-being.

To discern how to love our neighbors as ourselves, we need to begin with loving ourselves. The Torah commandment on which Jesus drew may not have meant that we should love our neighbors as much as we love ourselves. It may have meant something more along the lines of loving our neighbors as though we could not imagine seeing ourselves as separate from those neighbors. That said, loving our neighbors as ourselves today must start with loving ourselves, which means striving for our own flourishing. Denying ourselves well-being does not equip us either to have joyful lives filled with gratitude or to tend to the well-being of others effectively.

The Jewish sage Hillel the Elder (Hillel International 2017), who lived a few years before Jesus, famously said,

---

enemies benefit from inequality or injustice that causes us to suffer. For example, queer people do not need to prioritize the comfort of heterosexuals over their own well-being; women do not need to prioritize the comfort of men over their own well-being; and members of BIPOC communities do not need to prioritize the comfort of white people over their own well-being. Balancing our own well-being with the well-being of others is complicated and demands careful discernment. We are better equipped to carry out that discernment if we are committed to psychological and spiritual growth and to participation in communities of accountability. I discuss this issue further below and in later chapters.

"If I am not for myself, who will be for me? But if I am only for myself, what am I?" We can take both of these insights seriously, putting on our own oxygen mask before trying to help our neighbors put on their oxygen masks (as we are instructed at the beginning of plane flights). Striving for our own flourishing means taking steps to make sure that we have the capacity to thrive physically, emotionally, relationally, and in the other ways described here. It means advocating for our access to the preconditions of flourishing and it means taking actions to live into flourishing once those preconditions are in place. Striving for our own flourishing is lifelong aspirational work, made harder if we belong to devalued groups, have personal histories of trauma or mistreatment, or both. While it is not the only work that we must do in order to co-create God's kin-dom, it is part of the work. The more we love ourselves by tending to our own flourishing, the more we can commit to and actively support the flourishing of others.

Loving our neighbors as ourselves means working for the flourishing of our neighbors—those we know and those we do not know. This work, too, is extensive, complicated, lifelong, and aspirational. I presume that all people, without exception, are our neighbors (Luke 10:25–37). We are to show all people "mercy," which, in the context of the parable of the Good Samaritan, means mitigating their suffering through our care and resources. In the context of Jesus's other teachings and actions, we can include working for their flourishing along with mitigating their suffering as part of showing them mercy.

Finally, Jesus invites us to love our enemies, which may be the hardest thing we ever try to do. How on earth am I supposed to love people who carry out mass shootings in LGBTQ+ clubs (or schools or churches or movie theaters or offices)? How am I to love men who rape? How am I to love authoritarian dictators or warmongering politicians? How am I to love people who work actively to strip my rights from me? How am I to love people who lie about me and those I love in order to foment fear and hatred of people like us? How am I to love people who work tirelessly to block the flourishing of other people and who go to great effort to make other people suffer?

Here, connecting love with a commitment to human well-being offers a possible answer—not an easy answer, but certainly one that I find more plausible than most of the other answers I have encountered. I do not need to like my enemies or agree with their perspectives to love them. I do not need to wish them success in their harmful endeavors, and I certainly do not need to support their harmful endeavors. I do not even have to refrain from working against them politically. Loving my enemies requires me to desire and work for their flourishing, just as I desire and work for the flourishing of all other people.

Practically, loving my enemies demands that I put some of my time, energy, and resources toward being sure that they have access to the same preconditions of flourishing that I need, that those I love need, and that everyone I will never meet needs. My enemies must have the opportunity to flourish as embodied beings, emotional beings, relational beings, and in all the other ways that human beings can flourish, just as my friends and I must have that opportunity, and just as all people must have that opportunity.

I might act lovingly toward my enemies by working for the well-being of all human beings, with the understanding that such work will have a positive impact on my enemies. I might even choose to act specifically for my enemies' well-being, whether that means praying for them (Matthew 5:44) or doing something kind for one of them or a group of them (Luke 6:27–28).[2] It bears repeating: wanting my enemies to flourish does not mean wanting them to flourish at my expense or at anyone's expense. Praying for my enemies' well-being does not mean mistreating myself. Acting kindly toward someone who wishes me ill does not mean acting self-destructively or harming communities of which I am a part.

Loving my enemies means humanizing them even as they dehumanize me. It means refusing to mock them as they mock me, refusing to devalue them as they devalue me, refusing to harm them as they harm me. It does not require me to forgive them (though Jesus certainly invites me to do that). It simply, or not so simply, requires me to work for their well-being without any misapprehension that their well-being requires my suffering. *The well-being of my enemies does not require my suffering any more than my well-being requires their suffering.* If my enemies think differently on this point, Jesus's vision invites me to be confident that they are wrong, that each of us flourishes more fully when all of us flourish more fully.

Does loving my enemy in this sense mean that they are no longer my enemy? No—and yes. I may still be their enemy, someone against whom they conspire, someone they hate. I may also need to continue to acknowledge

---

2 Being uncomfortable can be part of flourishing, especially when our personal or spiritual growth or our work for justice demands some degree of discomfort on our parts. Wanting my enemies to flourish does not necessarily require my wanting them to be comfortable. Just as I must be willing to wrestle with discomfort as a white person striving to work against racism in a white supremacist society, I can expect my sexist and heterosexist enemies to be uncomfortable as they come to understand that sexism and heterosexism are not God's will for anyone and as they come to work against these forms of inequality. Acknowledging the importance of their discomfort in this context is not the same as wishing for them to suffer avoidably.

them as my enemy insofar as they seek to cause me harm. Moreover, I can confidently resist and work against any harm that they try to cause me (or anyone else). However, if I work for my enemy's well-being, there is one sense in which they are no longer my enemy: I am no longer striving against them, only against the harm they cause.

This way of thinking about enemies may also allow us to acknowledge the ways in which we are enemies of other people even when such is not our intent. We all cause harm—to ourselves, to people we know, to people we never meet. I benefit from white supremacy as a white person in ways that cause harm to members of BIPOC communities, as much as I wish it were otherwise. Are members of those communities justified in struggling against white supremacy? Absolutely! Can they choose to struggle against white supremacy while wanting all people, including white people, to flourish? Dr. King would, I think, have answered affirmatively, as would activists like Loretta Ross today (Ross 2021). Similarly, I can work against sexism and heterosexism while striving to treat actively sexist and heterosexist people better than they treat me. One of the mysteries of the kin-dom is the possibility that human flourishing is not a zero-sum game.

The end of the apostle Paul's famous "love chapter" (1 Corinthians 13:13) reminds us that faith, hope, and love abide, and that the greatest of these is love. If we understand flourishing to be the goal of our ethical lives, and if we understand love as the process of working for human and planetary flourishing, we can take inspiration from Paul's words and orient our lives more deeply toward co-creating the kin-dom of God as a community of flourishing, both individually and collectively. The final two chapters of this book suggest ways we might go about that work.

6

Co-creating the Kin-dom of God: Our Individual Work

Love is deep attention and profound curiosity. Love is non-judgmental and unattached to outcomes. Love is present in the moment, not lost in the past or future. Love is mindfulness. Love is divine. But for most of us, much of the time, love is hard work. And that's why we go to the fitness center on Sunday. (Jim Burklo, Tenderly Calling, *2021, 22)*

It seems appropriate to start this chapter with a confession. My father taught me to enjoy US football.[1] He also taught me to loathe particular teams and their quarterbacks. Recently, while watching a game in which the quarterback I most despise was playing, I found myself hoping that the opposing team's defense would hit the quarterback hard enough to knock him out of the game, perhaps even out of football entirely.

1 That's not the confession as such, though I admit that US football is highly problematic in and of itself from a feminist, anti-racist, and peace-valuing perspective.

I'm not proud of this response, but I'm also not alone in having it. In chapter 3, I discussed moral exclusion—the processes by which we designate people or groups as outside the community of those who deserve to be treated well—as a function of systemic inequality, such as racism. In reality, most of us are tempted to exclude a wide range of people from our moral universe, not just members of socially devalued groups to which we do not belong. Our lists may include people with differing political, cultural, or religious identities, individuals we simply don't like, and quarterbacks of opposing teams—along with our actual enemies. When we give in to temptation and treat anyone as undeserving of flourishing, it can feel pretty good if we are being honest.

The temptation to tolerate or even celebrate the avoidable suffering of some people is not, however, simply a matter of individual human frailty; the societies in which we live play a role. We learn who and what society finds valuable as we grow up. If we live in a society that is better at hating, judging, and excluding than at loving, forgiving, and including, we learn that some people's well-being matters more than the well-being of others. We also learn that society will reward us for caring about the "right" (socially valued) people and not caring about the "wrong" (socially devalued) people. Over time, our individual limitations work together with these larger social processes to make it harder for us to prioritize the flourishing of all people. No wonder Jesus taught that the gate that leads to life is narrow and the road that leads to life is hard (Matthew 7:13–14).

We need, therefore, to be clear about just how difficult it is to lovingly co-create God's kin-dom of human flourishing, especially on a regular basis. This aspirational work makes demands on us that can feel impossible. We are called to discern when we need to prioritize the well-being of others over our own comfort, and then to act on that valuing of other people to the best of our ability. We are called to be generous when we are most afraid of scarcity, kind when we are most afraid of cruelty, and loving even toward those who hate and harm us. We are called to acknowledge our wrongdoing and make reparations (Ruttenberg 2022). We are called to make sacrifices when we have a great deal and others do not have enough.

These invitations can feel overwhelming, but there are steps we can take to become the kind of people who are able to respond to them. In this chapter, I discuss individual work we can do to develop the resilience and strength that will equip us to co-create the kin-dom as a community of flourishing. First, I suggest four key virtues (dispositions and capacities) that we can develop to help us work for flourishing and against avoidable suffering. I then observe that psychological healing work and spiritual formation (broadly defined) play an important role in developing those dispositions and capacities along with the resilience to stay faithful in our striving for the kin-dom. I consider the kinds of political preparation we need to do to work effectively against the moral exclusion at the heart of systemic inequality. I close with mention of some concrete ways we can act as individuals to support flourishing and work against avoidable suffering.

Given the story with which I started the chapter, it should be clear that I am neither an expert in virtuous living nor a particularly spiritually mature person. I struggle with the same challenges, distractions, and temptations as everyone else. Knowing this, I also recognize the importance of cultivating our virtues, healing our psychic wounds, and growing in faith—both for our own well-being and for our ability to support the well-being of others.

Cultivating Virtues for Flourishing

There are many virtues (dispositions and capacities) we might cultivate to help us build communities and societies of flourishing. I want to lift up four virtues that seem particularly important for us to develop: humility, compassion, courage, and generosity.

Humility is crucial if we are to stop excluding individuals and groups from our moral communities. Believing that we are better than other people makes it easier for us to ignore their sacred worth and not to care whether they flourish or not. Believing that we are inferior to other people can make it harder for us to prioritize our own well-being, especially if we have personal histories of trauma, belong to socially devalued groups, or both. Humility can be a way of understanding ourselves in relation to other people: all inherently equal to one another morally, all deserving of the opportunity to flourish, all part of a larger mystery in which we are equally valued and valuable.

There's another component of humility that, while less obvious, can help inform both our personal actions and our political priorities. No one's flourishing should require anyone else to suffer avoidably, yet we live in societies in which getting to live a good life is understood as a zero-sum game. Some people have enough, others have more than enough, others do not have anywhere near enough, and everyone is forced to compete against other people—such is the nature (and culture) of the capitalist system in which many of us live.

A deep commitment to the well-being of all people requires us to reject the acquisitive logic of this system and instead to willingly choose economic modesty—in the words of the old slogan, to live simply so that others might simply live.[2] For those of us who are doing fairly

2 This saying has been attributed to Gandhi and to Mother Teresa, among others.

well (or very well) in the current system, this may be an aspiration beyond what we can make ourselves live out. We can, however, work toward living in this direction. If we care enough about the flourishing of all people, we can redistribute some of our wealth and be sure that some of our income goes to support people who do not have the survival resources that would give them a real chance of flourishing. Our capacity to make these changes depends on whether we have developed the humility that enables us to see ourselves as equal to all other people and therefore to find extreme economic inequality morally unacceptable.

If love as I have defined it is a matter of action, *compassion* is the felt response that drives loving action, a sensitivity to the suffering of others that compels us to strive to end their suffering. In the synoptic Gospels, Jesus's compassion for the crowds and for individual people (blind men, the mother of a dead son) inspires his actions of teaching, feeding, healing, and restoring life (Matthew 14:14, 20:34; Mark 6:34, 8:2; Luke 7:15). In Jesus's parable of the prodigal son, the father sees his son returning home, is filled with compassion, and runs toward him to welcome him back (Luke 15:20). Being part of Jesus's program involves cultivating compassion.

To be compassionate is to be open and vulnerable enough to the suffering of others that we allow that suffering to disturb, impact, and change us—to get us out of our heads, to touch our hearts, and to knot our stomachs—with the result that we take concrete actions to ease the suffering we encounter.[3] Given the amount of

3 "Compassion" comes from a Latin term that means "suffering with." Interestingly, the Hebrew word for compassion is related to the Hebrew word for "womb" and conveys the feelings a mother has for her child as well as the care the mother provides for the child ("Compassion" n.d.). Today, we might say that when we have a compassionate response to someone's suffering, we feel it in our gut.

suffering around us, compassion can be hard-won and precarious. We may not be able to respond to suffering with compassion as often as we might wish. We can, however, work to cultivate compassion in ourselves through psychological healing work and spiritual formation. As progressive Christian pastor and blogger John Pavlovitz (2020) puts it, "that's what all my reading and prayer and ministering and living as a Christian have yielded: following Jesus should leave me more compassionate, not less."

Working for our own well-being and for the well-being of others requires *courage*, especially if we live in societies that do not value most of the people who live in them. We will often find ourselves pushing against social norms that encourage us to look out only for ourselves or to treat only certain people as valuable and worthy. When no one else speaks up, we will need to do so; when no one asks hard questions, we will need to ask them. When no one else shares their resources with those in need, that demand will fall to us if we have the resources. In this context, I understand courage as the capacity to act bravely on behalf of our own well-being or the well-being of others even when doing so frightens us. We do not need to be fearless; we only need to be willing to take risks on behalf of what is right. This is especially true when the right thing means helping someone, or some group, flourish, or working against their suffering, as when we who belong to valued groups put our bodies on the line between devalued people and those attacking them. Cultivating courage makes it more likely that we will act morally in the world even when we are afraid.

Finally, there are two ways of thinking about *generosity* that help us understand both why it is so important and why it is so difficult. We can understand *material generosity* as the inclination to share what we have with others in service of their well-being. Generosity involves rejecting selfishness and replacing a mindset of scarcity with one of abundance. Practically, generosity leads us to offer others our resources (including financial resources), time, energy, gifts, and talents. Such generosity requires self-discipline and in some cases self-sacrifice.

Cultivating *generosity of spirit* involves learning to see people as more than their worst attributes, beliefs, values, and actions; or as author Kirsten Powers (2021, 9) puts it, "seeing the divine spark in other people, no matter how you feel about them." The uncharitable feeling about that quarterback with which I began this chapter is the opposite of generosity of spirit. I do not need to root for his team to win (which is good, because that is beyond my capacity), but I do need to see him as a human being entitled to all the good things that I would wish for myself and those I love.

Generosity of spirit also entails humility. When we are generous of spirit, we acknowledge our own failings and limitations and we avoid succumbing to a dualistic mindset in which we are perfect heroes and those we dislike are evil villains. We may still disagree with someone's opinions, find their values troubling, and work against their actions (for example, in the political sphere) but we extend to them a measure of grace. Our values, beliefs, and actions may be different, but we are both human beings, and we should both have access to good lives.

Psychological Healing

Humility, compassion, courage, and generosity sound good on paper, but living into them can be profoundly difficult. However much we want to be humble, humility takes practice and our best opportunities to practice it often come at the worst possible times: when we are anxious, ashamed, overwhelmed, or otherwise caught up in discomfort. Similarly, a life of generosity involves being generous both when we feel we can afford to do so and when we feel we cannot. When we are afraid, acting courageously is harder; when we are numb, compassion may feel unattainable.

Committing to cultivating these and other traits in the service of flourishing means committing to our personal growth more broadly and working to transform ourselves over time so that we may transform society. Psychological healing and spiritual formation are two kinds of personal growth that will be important for many of us.[4]

Psychological healing (through therapy, twelve-step programs, or community support groups, for example) can help us become more resilient, flexible, and open-hearted, which is important for both our own flourishing and our support of the flourishing of others. How can we experience embodied flourishing if our bodies are shut down by unresolved trauma? How can we flourish emotionally if we are caught up in addictions or self-destructive behaviors? How can we flourish relationally if childhood experiences have made our adult relationships tenuous, fraught, or defensive? How can we flourish spiritually if we are consumed with shame or anxiety? Whatever our particular histories, the work of psychological healing expands our capacity for well-being. Committing to this work and doing it is a profound, if often profoundly difficult, act of self-love.

---

4 Both psychological healing and spiritual formation can also strengthen us in the face of suffering we experience as a result of systemic inequality. Neither process is a replacement for activism in the service of justice and the flourishing of all, but some of the harm caused to members of devalued groups by inequality and the moral exclusion it generates may be mitigated through psychological and spiritual development.

We can access the joy, patience, gentleness, and self-control that Paul referred to as the "fruit of the Spirit" (Galatians 5:22–23) more effectively when we are emotionally well. I say this not as someone who is emotionally well every minute of every day, but as someone who has increasing access to this wellness as a result of the healing work that I have done and continue to do.

As we gain the ability to flourish, we become better able to attend to the well-being of others. We can give of ourselves more freely if we experience the peace and spaciousness that comes with being able to meet our own emotional needs. We can tolerate the inevitable discomfort of living into Jesus's vision—no less countercultural today than it was two millennia ago—if we understand our own relationship with discomfort and know how to let it flow through us without running from it or fighting it. It is easier to cultivate humility, compassion, courage, and generosity when we start from the deep truth of our own inherent worth—a deep truth that so many of us need to relearn as a result of experiences that have harmed us.

Spiritual Formation Practices

In addition to psychological healing work, we can engage in spiritual formation practices to deepen our trust in the sacred and strengthen our moral capacities. Such practices include, but are not limited to, silent meditation and prayer in their many forms, study of Scripture and other sources of spiritual wisdom, engagement with nature or the arts, spiritual direction, communal worship, and connections with communities of accountability. If our spiritual formation processes are broad and holistic enough, they will support our psychological healing work and enhance our relationships with our bodies, emotions, morality, creativity, spirituality, and other human attributes. Spiritual practices can help us flourish more deeply and can equip us to support the flourishing of others.

Our spiritual formation can empower us to choose the good more often than not when the choice is before us. The peace and wonder, joy, gratitude, and restoration that we find in silence, prayer, and other rituals of love strengthen us for moral action and comfort us when we fail to do our best. They also remind us of our commitment to the mystery at the heart of all that is good and of our commitment to embodying that goodness in the world.

In the face of hatred, spiritual practices can help us act in love. In times of cruelty, such practices can help us act kindly. When selfishness and greed seem paramount, spiritual practices can help us act generously. In societies that reward power-mongering, such practices can help us live humbly and hospitably in service to others. In an era of injustice and lies, spiritual practices can help us prioritize justice and the truth. When authoritarianism and fascism are growing, such practices can help us stay committed to egalitarianism and democracy. Ultimately, spiritual practices orient us to the flourishing of all people and help us reject the temptations of ease when those temptations are offered only to the privileged few; they also help us develop self-control in the face of those desires that it would be better for us not to pursue.

Another way to think about the value of spiritual formation is to consider the two processions of Palm Sunday—Pilate's procession and Jesus's procession—not just as a historical moment in which two opposing reigns were on display (Borg and Crossan 2006), but as two opposing ways of being in the world that are always competing for our hearts, minds, spirits, and bodies. Violence and non-violence invite us to join their processions. Domination and servanthood ask us to take up their causes. Greed and generosity welcome us to their programs. Arrogance and humility, cruelty and kindness, hard-heartedness and compassion, judgment and forgiveness, hatred and love await our cries of "hosanna!" ("save us!"), but only one of these paths can save us, and it is not the way of Pilate. Spiritual formation can help us repent of (literally, turn away from) Pilate's procession and gift us with the strength to follow Jesus even when doing so is profoundly difficult.

In a sense, neither psychological healing nor spiritual formation are really done alone. Both kinds of commitments engage us with other people—therapists, clergy, spiritual directors, those in our congregations, accountability groups, family, and friends. Both kinds of commitments are, however, our individual work. Our psychological healing and our spiritual growth happen through our own efforts, some of which are solitary and may even be lonely.

Political Preparation: Getting Ready to Expand the Moral Community

As important as psychological healing and spiritual formation are, they are incomplete until we understand how our assumptions and actions facilitate systemic inequality, and until we learn how to change those assumptions and actions. As discussed in chapter 3, most of us tend to grant some people the benefit of the doubt while withholding it from others. When this happens in a large-scale, patterned way based on categories such as race, gender, and sexuality, we contribute to the blocked flourishing and avoidable suffering that come with white supremacy, sexism, heterosexism, and all forms of systemic inequality. As long as our assumptions and actions reproduce inequality, we are causing harm even when that is the last thing we want to do.

Fortunately, there are concrete steps we can take that will enable us to repent of our role in these forms of inequality. We can begin to educate ourselves about their history and present reality, taking stock of what we already know and asking what we need to learn next. We can work on getting comfortable with the discomfort of facing those forms of inequality from which we benefit, such as racism if we are white or sexism if we are male. We can start to monitor our own assumptions and actions to determine when, where, and how we are privileging some people and disadvantaging others in systemic ways. We can practice challenging those assumptions and we can imagine how we might change our actions. We can set about identifying ways to use our power, energy, time, and resources to support justice, which is to say, to support human well-being.

As we come to understand how we ourselves are implicated in these forms of inequality, we gain the ability to imagine and then to co-create a world with far more flourishing and far less avoidable suffering—one assumption at a time and one action at a time.

Taking Action for Flourishing and against Suffering

Beyond the work we do to prepare or equip ourselves for loving service to the world, we act individually as well as with others to support flourishing and to diminish avoidable suffering. We support our friends, family members, and other loved ones during good times and challenging times. We provide food to hungry people, visit prisoners, donate money to organizations that support or advocate for devalued communities, strive to minimize our environmental footprint, vote for "pro-flourishing" and "anti-suffering" politicians, and otherwise engage in individual activities to enhance human and planetary well-being and to limit suffering.

These actions are distinct from psychological healing and spiritual formation work. We probably carried them out before attending to our psychological and spiritual development and will continue to carry them out as we grow individually. Neither our internal work nor our service to the world is ever done, and while we might focus on them separately or simultaneously, they will inform one another. As we heal and grow, we become better equipped to support flourishing and challenge suffering in the world; as we make a broader difference, we identify new ways to become stronger and kinder.

Individual work is necessary but not sufficient if we want to co-create the kin-dom of God as a community of flourishing. Chapter 7 addresses some of the work we do with others to make Jesus's vision a reality.

7

Co-creating the Kin-dom of God: Our Collective Work

The reign of God is about doing for the entire human family what we do within our individual families. Loving the whole human family means insuring that everyone gets a fair and equitable access to the necessary means of life: food, clean water, clothing, shelter, education, health care, meaningful employment, safety, and protection from violence. As followers of Jesus, it is up to us to figure out how to live together as a human community, how to love one another, and how to care for the earth and all its creatures. (Kurt Struckmeyer, A Conspiracy of Love, *2016, 199)*

If we are to "dream God's dream"[1] of a world of flourishing and then make that dream a reality, we have a lot of work before us, and much of that work is collective. We can prepare for our role in the work individually, and we can make the world a kinder, more joyous, more loving place individually; however, because so many of the situations that block flourishing and cause avoidable suffering are systemic, our only hope of substantial, large-scale change

1 Again, I am indebted to progressive Christian songwriter Bryan Sirchio both for this phrase and for permission to use it in this book.

is in our communal labor to reimagine what is possible and then bring it into being.

While we will work with people from other religious traditions and with those outside of religion to co-create this world of flourishing, those of us committed to following Jesus as progressive Christians are not merely trying to make the world better because we agree that the world ought to be better (as much as we do agree with this claim). We are also trying to embody God's realm of love among us as Jesus described it, a community of wholeness, wellness, flourishing, abundance, and shalom.

Pastor and professor Christopher Grundy points out that "the Beloved Community is deeply rooted in the biblical concept of shalom: the social, political, economic, even ecological well-being or flourishing of all of creation" (2019, 174). Similarly, author Jason Porterfield offers a beautiful account of this vision:

> Shalom denotes more than just the absence of violence. It indicates harmony, health, and wholeness in all aspects of life. Shalom exists when all our relationships are flourishing: our relationship with God, with each other, with creation, and even with ourselves. It is the state in which everything is as it ought to be . . . This vision of peace is profoundly comprehensive in scope. It leaves no aspect of life untouched. And it can never coexist with injustice. This is the kind of peace that Jesus . . . calls his followers to also actively advance. (Porterfield 2022, 24–25)

Whatever else progressive Christianity is, it ought to be a social change movement for human and planetary flourishing. This movement should be built on individual and collective spiritual practices, support and accountability from our co-conspirators, and courageous, selfless work in the world. We are called to take care of the politically disenfranchised, the economically exploited and marginalized, and the socially devalued, as well as to resist the systems responsible for the disenfranchising, exploitation, marginalization, and devaluation.[2] In this chapter, I briefly revisit the importance of justice as a concept that will inform our work, suggest some current arenas in which we might work for human well-being, and end by reflecting on how our commitment to societal well-being might lead us to reshape our congregations as what progressive Christian pastor and author Jim Burklo calls spiritual "fitness centers."

Revisiting Justice

In chapter 1, I claimed that basing our ethics on justice could be problematic because that term has been used in the service of very different goals, some of which promote flourishing and some of which cause avoidable suffering. If, however, we understand the pursuit of justice as a way to reach the goal of extending flourishing to all people rather than as a goal in itself, justice returns to being the prophetic principle spoken of and lived into by Jesus, his ancestors, and his followers.

It is telling that justice can be understood as a form of love. Cornel West (1989, 271) famously said that justice is what love looks like in public. Ethicist Joseph Fletcher (1966, 87) claimed that "love and justice are the same, for justice is love distributed, nothing else," while ethicist Marvin Ellison (1996, 14) refers to "justice-love." Dr. King

---

2 An earlier articulation of the idea that progressive Christians should resist harmful systems (Cobb 2008) addressed consumerism, economic inequality, American imperialism, and global climate change, among other topics.

(2010, 38) drew a similar connection in commenting that "power without love is reckless and abusive, and love without power is sentimental and anemic. Power at its best is love implementing the demands of justice, and justice at its best is power correcting everything that stands against love." Biblical scholars Marcus Borg and John Dominic Crossan (2006, 215) claim that "love is the soul of justice, and justice is the body, the flesh, of love." Given a definition of love as the work we do to flourish in all aspects of our lives and to help all other people flourish in all aspects of their lives (as discussed in chapter 5), we might understand our commitment to justice as a commitment to love people we will never meet. In what follows, I use the term in this way.

Justice Work as Work for Flourishing

We may already know where we want to put our time, energy, resources, and bodies in the service of justice. Some of us may focus on anti-democratic initiatives such as voter suppression or the rise of authoritarian white Christian nationalism. Some of us may prioritize peacemaking, working against environmental degradation, or supporting suffering people in other countries. I personally prioritize working against US anti-Black racism (as a white person who benefits from white supremacy), attacks on the rights of women and LGBTQ+ people (as a queer woman), and intersections of those areas. We may or may not already think about our justice work in relation to human flourishing, though we surely grieve the human suffering that inspires our response as we carry out this work.

The ethic of flourishing developed in part 1 may or may not change our justice commitments, but it may give us new language to make sense of what drives our work or even suggest new directions for our activism.

For example, if we are particularly concerned about embodied flourishing, the preconditions discussed in chapter 5 suggest many potential priorities for us, including the following:

As embodied beings, we need access to survival resources, including clothes, shelter, nutritious and safe food, clean water, clean air, and sanitary environments to be able to flourish. We can support access to survival resources for all by working against environmental racism, poverty and economic inequality,[3] and hiring and workplace discrimination. Similarly, we can work for food and housing for all people and for jobs that pay living wages in all industries. We can be part of efforts to address air pollution, water pollution, and other environmental degradation and to prevent further despoiling of the earth.

We also need access to appropriate, comprehensive, and affordable healthcare, which suggests working against healthcare discrimination (by race, gender, sexuality, socioeconomic status, and religion, for example) and for a universal healthcare system that is not tied to one's place of employment. Even in the absence of universal healthcare, we might work for free or inexpensive and widely available vaccines and other preventative health measures, as well as for affordable medications.

We need to be safe from physical and sexual violence and other kinds of harm, such as workplaces that do not prioritize the safety of employees. Knowing this, we may choose to work against sexual assault, antigay or anti-trans violence, police violence (especially against members of BIPOC communities and people with mental health challenges), or the death penalty (widely known to be applied in racist ways[4]). We may focus on workplace safety or on

3 See Desmond 2023.

4 Balko 2020; Death Penalty Information Center 2020; Ndulue 2020; Phillips and Marceau 2020.

restorative justice alternatives to our current, undeniably violent criminal justice system. More broadly, since Jesus pronounced the peacemakers blessed (Matthew 5:9), we might strive for peaceful alternatives to war.

We need control over how we use our bodies and what happens to them, which might lead us to work for safe, legal, affordable contraception and abortion access, for the right of trans people to obtain the medical care they need, and for broader economic justice that would afford people more options about how they use their bodies. We also might be inspired to work for body-positive lifespan sex education in schools and religious settings so that all people better understand both the possibilities and the challenges of being a sexual person.

Since all forms of flourishing have preconditions, there are many possible places to start in supporting human flourishing and working against avoidable suffering. Here, I suggest only a few additional examples:

If we are concerned about emotional flourishing, we must be concerned about all forms of systemic discrimination, about bullying, street harassment, and racial profiling, and about all forms of physical and sexual violence that cause trauma and emotional harm (which is to say, all of them).

If we are concerned about relational flourishing, we may want to be advocates for people estranged from their families or communities for reasons of sexuality, gender identity, or changes in religious identities (among other possible examples).

If we are concerned about meaning-making flourishing, we will challenge racist, sexist, heterosexist, and otherwise harmful messages that come from religious leaders, politicians, cultural icons such as performers and athletes, teachers, and others with influence over how people see the world.

If we are concerned about agentic flourishing, we will find systemic denial of some people's autonomy and political power unacceptable, which may lead us to oppose voter suppression efforts, anti-trans laws, and authoritarian, anti-democratic movements. Agentic flourishing also requires both safety and access to the resources, opportunities, and experiences that allow us to pursue our goals. This covers a range of arenas for social change, some of which are discussed above under embodied flourishing.

If we are concerned about flourishing as learning beings, we will want to oppose the widespread movement to pass laws restricting teaching about sexuality, gender identity, and any aspect of race in the US that makes white people uncomfortable. If we work in academia, we will also want to take steps to minimize problematic assumptions about who can succeed in the classroom and to strive to prevent stereotype threat (Steele 2010). We may work against the criminalization of BIPOC children and the sexualization of young girls.

As for the work itself, it is likely to include a mix of self-education, individual actions on behalf of the causes we care about (voting, donating money, writing letters to the editor, joining public protests, educating our friends and families), joining in solidarity with social change movements addressing the same issues, and using whatever decision-making authority we have within institutions to support the disenfranchised, exploited, marginalized, and devalued. In the context of this chapter, the work we do as part of larger social change movements is crucial; none of us can change entrenched systems of harm by ourselves. For many of us, this work is not new but framing it in terms of expanding human flourishing, particularly in light of the specific attributes discussed here, may inspire us in ways we cannot yet predict, whether in the actions we take or in the ways we try to convince others to join with us.

Church as Spiritual "Fitness Center"

We go to church for many reasons, not all of which have to do with maximizing human flourishing across society and the planet. That said, if we bring an ethic of flourishing into our congregational life, church may offer us even more effective nourishment for the difficult labor of co-creating the kin-dom of flourishing.

What might we find, for example, if we committed to reading the Bible as a source of wisdom about human well-being and the things that interfere with it, or as a guide to communal spiritual practices that can strengthen us for the work ahead? How would our worship rituals change if we were intentional about tying them more directly to our commitment to building communities of flourishing?[5] How might both worship and faith formation (such as Bible study) serve to reorient us or recommit us to these values and the actions that follow from them? How can our practices of repentance and confession incorporate understandings about how we are complicit in systems of avoidable suffering? What if we took Jim Burklo's language about church as a "fitness center" seriously? What muscles are we building in church and how are we building them? How are we strengthening ourselves for moral living and nourishing ourselves in deepening trust and joy?

Jesus lived a radically hospitable life. In our gathering to remember and learn from his life, we have opportunities to practice radical hospitality ourselves. Congregational life might become, among other things, an opportunity to practice generosity among ourselves in new ways as well as a laboratory of radical hospitality for those who are currently outside our doors or who are within them but quietly alienated. Such practice may take many forms,

---

5 For an approach to Communion that centers harm reduction and integrates Jesus's pro-flourishing work more fully, see Grundy 2019.

from assuring that spaces are truly accessible to people with mobility limitations or physical disabilities to offering gluten-free bread and grape juice at Communion. The ideas that follow presume that congregations have room to deepen their current practices of hospitality, but are not meant to presume that (for example) congregations are entirely white, heterosexual, or able-bodied.

One opportunity to practice generosity comes with the fact that, for those of us in smaller congregations with different age groups, there is likely no way to program worship music that all congregants will find equally meaningful and nourishing at all times; some of us will prefer modern worship music and others will prefer traditional hymns.[6] This diversity of perspectives is a tremendous opportunity for all of us to agree joyfully that the music that moves some of us less should be included regularly in worship if it moves other people more. We can all become willing to engage with some worship music that is less meaningful to us personally but more meaningful to those we care about in the next seat or pew. Understood as a practice of generosity, this way of engaging with worship music can enrich all of us over time.

Congregations can develop worship practices that are fully inclusive of children, people with mental illnesses, members of BIPOC communities, women, and LGBTQ+ people. The language congregations use in their liturgy and sacred music can clarify that whoever and whatever

---

6 As a hymnwriter and sacred music composer myself, I tend to be moved by progressive Christian songs currently being written by (for example) members of the Convergence Music Project (https://www.convergencemp.com/), while the older members of my congregation are moved by the hymns of the late nineteenth century with which they grew up. Every Sunday, I play a mix of both types of music and am comforted to know that some of what I play nourishes and inspires me while the rest of it nourishes and inspires my older friends in the congregation.

else God is, God is not an old, putatively heterosexual, able-bodied white man—that people of all ages, genders, racial backgrounds, abilities, and sexualities are made in the image of God. Congregations can similarly make a point of showcasing artwork (including nativity scenes) from around the world.

Congregations can incorporate sacred music from different cultures and traditions as long as this is done respectfully and thoughtfully, providing information and context about the music with congregants. Predominantly or entirely white congregations that sing music written by African American composers can commit to contributing money to racial justice organizations when such music is used—a form of "musical reparation." Congregations can also consider whether similar reparation practices might make sense when using certain pieces of international music or Indigenous American music.

Congregations can celebrate Trans Visibility Day and the Trans Day of Remembrance. They can celebrate Pride Month, Black History Month, Native American Heritage Month, and Women's History Month—all year long. They can engage in interfaith community building, as long as this is done carefully and thoughtfully. Congregations can use their worship spaces to host unhoused people, especially when weather conditions make it dangerous for such people to remain outside overnight.

The opportunities for radical hospitality in our congregations are limited only by our knowledge and our imaginations, and we can commit to extending our knowledge and opening our imaginations continuously over time. Jesus used parables to invite people into a surprising new way of understanding God's dream for humanity. We can use our congregations in similar ways, and in doing so, expand our own flourishing and the flourishing of those around us.

We have covered a lot of ground in these chapters. I have proposed a way of thinking about ethics that may be new to people, considered its implications for addressing systemic inequality, explored precursors to this way of thinking in the Bible, and contemplated what God, love, and flourishing might have to do with one another. In these final two chapters, I have suggested how we might work on transforming ourselves and how we might think about transforming society to co-create the kin-dom envisioned by Jesus as a community of flourishing. Since I began the introduction with a nightmare, it only remains to conclude the book with a dream—our best interpretation of God's dream for us and our world.

Conclusion

> *You have been waiting for God, [Jesus] said, while God has been waiting for you. No wonder nothing is happening. You want God's intervention, he said, while God wants your collaboration. God's [kin-dom] is here, but only insofar as you accept it, enter it, live it, and thereby establish it. (John Dominic Crossan,* The Power of Parable, *2012, 127)*

Imagine a world in which all people flourished. Imagine all people freed and empowered to be and become their best selves, to pursue their callings, to offer their gifts to a world that wanted those gifts and appreciated them, to take in the gifts of others in delight and thankfulness.

Imagine all people at home and at ease in their bodies, fearless, gentle, strong, secure in the knowledge that they were safe from violence, danger, and harm wherever they found themselves. Imagine all people knowing that they would never lack for survival resources.

Imagine all people unafraid of their emotional lives because they knew they were capable of handling even the toughest emotions they faced and that they would have the support of others in such moments.

Imagine all people knowing that they were loved and capable of loving, unafraid to be dependent on other people and fully prepared to build their lives interdependently with those around them. Imagine all people knowing that they could be their full selves with their families and friends without any fear of rejection.

Imagine all people able to make sense of their experiences in ways that opened their hearts and restored their spirits. Imagine all people being able to tell their stories knowing that others were listening respectfully and with interest. Imagine all people being well and whole enough to cherish and prioritize listening to the stories of others.

Imagine all people able to use their self-efficacy for good, making a positive difference in the world and leaving a legacy that would long be remembered.

Imagine all people able to grow and learn over the course of their lives, unafraid of making mistakes, free to become more knowledgeable, more competent, more humble, more connected.

Imagine all people navigating society in comfort and with confidence, knowing that they would be treated well wherever they went.

Imagine all people able to act out of their best moral intuitions in societies that rewarded moral behavior and helped people repair harm when, as will inevitably happen, people made mistakes.

Imagine all people able to access their creativity and generate new ideas, things, and relationships out of that creativity, inspired by their full and free access to the creativity of others.

Imagine all people able to experience awe, reverence, wonder, and a sense of being part of something larger than themselves.

Imagine non-human creation restored to wellness and wholeness. Imagine clean air and water, a reversal of global climate change, a newly deepened relationship with the other beings with whom we share the planet.

What would it be like to live in a world of flourishing, a world so different from the world in which we live now? For me, the words that come to mind are peace, joy, and gratitude. Perhaps those are the words that you thought of, or perhaps this exercise evoked something else in you. Either way, I find it a beautiful image and hope you do as well.

We are not restricted merely to imagining this world of abundance. We can work toward making it a reality. We are, in fact, called to make it a reality. To borrow biblical scholar John Dominic Crossan's language, quoted in the epigraph to this conclusion, we are called to "accept [this reality], enter it, live it, and thereby establish it."

What, then, are we to do? We are to feed the hungry, free the prisoner, tend to the least valued in society, and support the sick. We are to throw feasts and invite everyone. We are to do whatever psychological and spiritual work we need to do to understand and accept that we ourselves are loved, lovable and loving, whatever our frailties and challenges. We are to tend to our own flourishing—physically, emotionally, socially, morally, and in all other ways. We are to tend to each other's flourishing—physically, emotionally, socially, morally, and in all other ways. We are to remake society so that every single person has a real chance to flourish—physically, emotionally, socially, morally, and in all other ways. We are to care for creation so that all non-human beings have a chance to flourish in whatever context that is possible for them.

And we are to do all of this in memory of Jesus, because this work is our best understanding of what he would have wanted. We are to be Jesus in the world today. This is a daunting demand, so we gather to help each other remember this demand and practice living it out. We gather to support each other and cheer each other on, and to help each other when we are struggling. The details of the work of flourishing are specific to our time and the language we use to talk about how to do this work is similarly contemporary, but the value behind this work—the vision behind this work—is nothing less than the kin-dom of God as Jesus imagined it.

Taking up and living out an ethic of flourishing can ultimately be understood as a particular way of following Jesus, a path involving both deep joy and substantial self-sacrifice as we cultivate delight and strenuously develop such virtues as courage, generosity, humility, and compassion. Perhaps such an ethic, if taken seriously by enough people, would contribute to moving all of us and our planet toward lives more abundant than we can imagine today. It's hard to know, but I remain hopeful even in these profoundly challenging times. After all, as we have been taught, nothing is impossible with love.

"A Creed of Love" by Kurt Struckmeyer

We believe in the hidden God of love:
the spirit of love and compassion found at the breadth
and depth of every human life.
We believe in the vision of Jesus:
the reigning of God on earth, found where people
and societies are governed by the rule of love.
We believe in the way of Jesus:
a love for God and neighbor, a love for stranger and enemy,
a love for the outcast and alien.
We believe in the abundant life of Jesus:
a life of acceptance, inclusion, and forgiveness,
a life of equality, generosity, and sharing,

a life of compassion, service, and nonviolence.
We believe that Jesus modeled the godly life:
healing the sick and serving the poor, seeking dignity and equality for all people, and calling for shared wealth and economic justice.
For this he was condemned and crucified by those who serve the forces of domination in every time and place.
We believe that though he died, the spirit of Jesus lives on among those who strive for peace and justice
and who work to create a better world.
In the name of Jesus, and in the name of love,
we commit ourselves to care for others,
to break down the barriers that separate us,
and to seek justice and peace in the world.

Questions for Discussion Groups

Introduction

1. What beliefs about ethics and morality are you bringing to this book? When and where did you learn them? From whom? Are your current beliefs about ethics and morality the same as those you had as a younger person or have your beliefs changed over time?
2. The author observes that "the tragedy and beauty of humanity was on full display" at a memorial site to the victims of a mass shooting. When and where have you seen "the tragedy and beauty of humanity" joined

together? How did those experiences make you feel? What did you learn from them?

3. Consider the description of progressive Christians, taken from ProgressiveChristianity.org. Based on this description, would you consider yourself a progressive Christian? Why or why not?
4. The Introduction offers some preliminary thoughts about the author's "ethic of flourishing." How do you feel about this approach to ethics so far? What do you think about it?

Chapter 1. From Principles to People

1. The author claims that rights and freedom are problematic bases for ethics because the concepts can be used to justify actions that harm people as well as actions that help people. Have you experienced these terms or others like them (justice, equality) being used in harmful ways? In positive ways?
2. The author provides a broad and a more specific definition of human flourishing. When you think about flourishing (or well-being, thriving, or getting to have a good life), what does that look like and feel like for you?
3. The author claims that we should "treat people rather than principles as the point of ethics." She also claims that the moral goodness of an idea or action (for example) has to do with whether it supports human well-being. How might your life be different if more people approached ethics in this way?
4. The author claims that there is a difference between the suffering that is part of having a good life and what she terms "avoidable suffering." Have you experienced suffering that is part of having a good life? Have you

experienced "avoidable suffering"? How are they different in your experience?

5. At the end of the chapter, the author introduces ten human attributes: embodiment, emotions, relationality, meaning-making, sociality (being part of society), agency, learning, morality, creativity, and spirituality. What are some experiences you've had in which one or more of these attributes played an important positive or negative role?

Chapter 2. Our Common Humanity

1. The author describes the human attributes mentioned above in this chapter. Where did you see your own experiences captured in these descriptions?
2. Given that the discussion of these attributes is fairly brief, are there other points that you would want to add? Based on your own experiences, is there more to say about embodiment or any other attribute that helps you understand its importance in human life?
3. The author claims that people are simultaneously human beings with universal human attributes, individuals with unique experiences, and members of differently valued social groups. Where do you see this complexity in your life? For example, are there times when you feel more like an individual or more like a member of a social group?
4. The author claims that people are simultaneously dependent on others throughout their lives, interdependent in co-creating social life, and independent in having the ability to take action as individuals. Where do you see this complexity in your life? When and how are you dependent? Interdependent? Independent?

5. The author takes an expansive approach to creativity. Where do you encounter creativity in your own life (whether in the more traditional sense of the term or in this expansive usage)?
6. The author similarly defines spirituality in a broad way and notes that spirituality does not need to be connected to organized religion, though it can be. When and where have you had spiritual experiences (broadly defined)? In what contexts or situations do you feel a part of something larger than yourself?
7. The author notes that because human attributes intersect in our lives, it is possible to flourish across multiple attributes at the same time ("integrated flourishing") but also to suffer across multiple attributes at the same time ("aggravated suffering"). Have you experienced integrated flourishing or aggravated suffering? If so, what has that been like for you?
8. What concrete actions could you take to support your own flourishing in terms of one or more of these attributes? To support the flourishing of other people?

Chapter 3. Flourishing, Suffering, and Inequality

1. The author suggests a way of thinking about systemic inequality based on people being given the benefit of the doubt or having the benefit of the doubt withheld from them, both in institutional contexts and in public life. Have you ever received or been denied the benefit of the doubt based on a social group to which you belonged? How did that experience make you feel? How did it change the way you thought about other people?
2. The author introduces the notion of "moral exclusion," the processes and practices by which some people are defined as outside the community of those who

deserve to be treated morally. Have you ever felt as though you were being morally excluded? How did that experience make you feel?

3. The author suggests that there are four types of preconditions of flourishing: (1) access to resources, experiences, and opportunities that support flourishing, (2) safety (freedom from harm, trauma, mistreatment, violence, and danger), (3) autonomy and self-determination, and (4) respect and positive treatment by individuals and larger social groups. The author claims that members of devalued groups cannot count on those kinds of preconditions being available to them, making it harder for them to flourish. Have you ever been in a situation in which you did not have access to one or more of these types of preconditions? How did that experience make you feel?
4. The author ultimately claims that a moral commitment to the well-being of all people necessarily invites us to work against systemic inequality. What do you think of this claim? How does it make you feel?
5. What concrete actions could you take to ease the avoidable suffering or improve the flourishing of members of a devalued group to which you yourself do not belong? A devalued group to which you do belong?

Chapter 4. Jesus, the Prophets, and Beyond

1. The author claims that while Jesus did not use the term "flourishing" to our knowledge, his words and actions show him to have been concerned with human well-being. Which of the author's examples make this point most compellingly for you? Are there other Gospel passages you would add that make the same point?

2. The author draws a connection between Micah 6:8 (in the context of Micah 6:6–7) and Jesus's two great commandments. Does bringing these two passages together help you understand either in new ways? If so, how?
3. Beyond the passages from James and the Acts of the Apostles, can you think of other New Testament materials that support the idea that early Christian communities were committed to the flourishing of their members (particularly the poor)?
4. Which New Testament passages are the most meaningful to you? Why? Do any of them suggest anything about the importance of human well-being to Jesus and his earliest followers?

Chapter 5. Love, Flourishing, and God

1. The author defines love as "the work we do to flourish in all aspects of our lives and to help all other people flourish in all aspects of their lives." How is this definition of love different from your current understanding of love? How is it similar?
2. The author suggests that we can love ourselves and others by guaranteeing that we and they have access to certain preconditions of flourishing. What do you think of this suggestion? How does it make you feel?
3. The author suggests that we might understand God (among our many other understandings of God) as "incarnated and made manifest as love in the work we do and the relationships we build in support of our own flourishing and the flourishing of others." How do you feel about the idea that our work for flourishing embodies the sacred? Does this idea move you? Excite you? Disturb you? What other responses do you have?

4. The author claims that loving our enemies requires us to "desire and work for their flourishing, just as [we] desire and work for the flourishing of all other people." How do you feel about this claim? Does it move you? Excite you? Disturb you? What other responses do you have?

Chapter 6. Co-creating the Kin-dom of God: Our Individual Work

1. The author begins the chapter with a story in which she experiences a morally ugly impulse. What are some of your morally ugly impulses? How do you keep from acting on them?
2. The author suggests four virtues that are particularly important to cultivate if we are to contribute to building God's kin-dom as a community of flourishing: humility, compassion, courage, and generosity. How are these virtues important to you? How are you cultivating them in your life? What other virtues are important to you, and why?
3. The author suggests that psychological healing work can support us in developing the virtues mentioned above as well as helping us cultivate the resilience we need to do the work of the kin-dom. If you have engaged in psychological healing work, what have you done and how has it helped you? What kinds of psychological healing work might you pursue in the future?
4. The author suggests that spiritual formation can similarly help us cultivate the virtues and resilience we need to co-create the kin-dom. What kinds of spiritual formation activities have you practiced in the past? What kinds are you practicing now? How are they helping you grow spiritually?

5. The author suggests individual actions we can take to support the flourishing of others. What kinds of individual actions do you take to make the world a better place?

Chapter 7. Co-creating the Kin-dom of God: Our Collective Work

1. The author claims that progressive Christianity ought to be (among other things) "a social change movement for human and planetary flourishing." How do you feel about this claim?
2. The author says that we might consider our commitment to justice "a commitment to love people we will never meet." How do you feel about this idea? How do you think love and justice are connected to each other?
3. Using embodied flourishing as the primary example, the author draws connections between preconditions of flourishing and a number of justice, peace, and environmental initiatives. Which of these initiatives, if any, are you involved with now? Are there other preconditions of flourishing that are important to you? What justice, peace, and/or environmental initiatives might connect with those preconditions?
4. The author suggests questions that congregations can ask themselves to help them focus on issues of flourishing. If you belong to a congregation, how might your congregation answer these questions? What steps might your congregation take over time to become more centered on human or planetary flourishing?
5. The author suggests concrete ways in which congregations can practice generosity and hospitality. If you belong to a congregation, is your congregation already

engaged with any of these practices? Which ones sound like good candidates for consideration?

Conclusion

1. The author invites readers to imagine a world of flourishing, providing specific examples. As you reflect on the book as a whole, what images come to mind when you try to imagine a world of flourishing? How do those images make you feel?
2. The author believes that Jesus would have wanted us to flourish and to help others flourish. How does this way of thinking about Jesus make you feel?
3. Do you believe that nothing is impossible with love? How might your life change if you acted as though it were true (whether you believe it or not)?

Acknowledgments

Thanks to Rev. David Felten for writing the foreword. Thanks to Bryan Sirchio for permission to reproduce the chorus of his song “Dream God’s Dream.”

Thanks to Deborah Grady for permission to reprint the 2022 version of the “Core Values of Progressive Christianity” from the ProgressiveChristianity.org website.

Thanks to Brian Hehn for permission to use a quote from an email to Hymn Society members.

Thanks to Kurt Struckmeyer for permission to reproduce his “Creed of Love” as it appears in the video “A Conspiracy of Love #20: Rev. David Felten in conversation with author Kurt Struckmeyer."

My ethic of flourishing has been in development for over a decade. I am profoundly grateful to High Plains Church Unitarian Universalist (Colorado Springs, CO), Flame of Life Universalists (Pueblo, CO), Heather Powell Browne, Rev. John Churcher and the St. Albans group of the Progressive Christianity Network Britain, Jan Edwards, Dr. Re Evitt, Dr. Peony Fhagen, and Tess Powers for offering me forums in which to share and refine these concepts.

Dr. Helen Daly has been my primary conversation partner about ethical matters. Her patience and kindness continue to amaze me.

Dr. Phoebe Lostroh and Maggie Jusell beta read the entire book and improved it tremendously. I cannot thank them enough. Other helpful input came from Deb Donley, Martha Hoffman, and Pastor Steve Osborn.

Brian Allain, Rev. Tisha Brown, Rev. Erin Gilmore, Rev. Melissa Guthrie, Dr. Dennis McEnnerney, Rev. Brian McLaren, Rev. Paul Turner, Dr. Barbara Whitten, and far too many Facebook friends to mention have supported this project. Thank you so much.

Deep thanks to Rev. Andy DeBraber for connecting me with The Pilgrim Press after my initial publisher was unable to complete the book, and of course to Rev. Rachel Hackenberg, Katie Martin, Adam Bresnahan, David Grandouiller, Rev. Vanessa Myers-Dudley, and George Thomas.

Many pastors, musicians, writers, and fellow seekers have enriched my spiritual life, inspired me, and pushed me to keep seeking the good. I'm sorry I cannot list everyone who should be included here. Those I absolutely must thank by name include Rev. Jim Burklo, Rev. Richard Bruxvoort Colligan, Rev. Mallory Everhart, Rev. David Felten, Rev. Dr. Christopher Grundy, Rev. Abby Henrich,

Rev. Kelly Kahlstrom, Spencer LaJoye, Eric McEuen, Rev. Julia McKay, Frank Metzger, Rev. Jeff Proctor-Murphy, Rev. Mollie Ronge, Rev. Bryan Sirchio, Kurt Struckmeyer, Rev. Deborah Tinsley, Rev. Clare Twomey, and the people of Vista Grande Community Church UCC (Colorado Springs, CO). I am who I am today because of many people, but I can say with certainty that this book would not exist without the insights, strength, and hope that I have gained from you. In your differing ways, you have shown me what sacred love can look like (and sound like) as it is embodied in human form. My thanks beyond words to you all.

And, of course, my undying gratitude to the sacred mystery that we call by many names and that cannot possibly be reduced to one name or to a thousand. May I—may we all—come to know you and live in you even as you live in and through us.

Bibliography

Allison, Dorothy. *Skin: Talking about Sex, Class, and Literature.* Ithaca, NY: Firebrand Books, 1994.

Bailey, Zinzi D., Nancy Krieger, Madina Agénor, Jasmine Graves, Natalia Linos, and Mary T. Bassett. "Structural Racism and Health Inequities in the USA: Evidence and Interventions." *Lancet* 389, no. 10077 (April 2017): 1453–1463.

Balko, Radley. "There's Overwhelming Evidence that the Criminal-Justice System is Racist. Here's the Proof." *Washington Post*, June 10, 2020. https://www.washingtonpost.com/graphics/2020/opinions/systemic-racism-police-evidence-criminal-justice-system/.

Ball, Carlos. *The Morality of Gay Rights: An Exploration in Political Philosophy*. New York: Routledge, 2003.

Bass, Diana Butler. "The Kin-dom of God." Red Letter Christians, December 15, 2021. https://www.redletterchristians.org/the-kin-dom-of-god/.

Bauer, Nichole M. *The Qualifications Gap: Why Women Must be Better than Men to Win Political Office*. New York: Cambridge University Press, 2020.

BBC. "How Many US Mass Shootings Have There Been in 2023?" BBC, April 16, 2023. https://www.bbc.com/news/world-us-canada-41488081.

Bedick, Barry R. "Categories of Laws Involving Marital Status/Tables of Laws in the United States Code Involving Marital Status, by Category." U.S. General Accounting Office, January 31, 1997. https://www.gao.gov/archive/1997/og97016.pdf.

Berdyaev, Nicolas. *The Destiny of Man*. New York: Harper Torchbooks, 1960.

Borg, Marcus J., and John Dominic Crossan. *The Last Week: What the Gospels Really Teach about Jesus's Final Days in Jerusalem*. New York: HarperOne, 2006.

Burklo, Jim. *Tenderly Calling: An Invitation to the Way of Jesus*. Haworth, NJ: St. Johann Press, 2021.

Clawson, Laura. "GOP Congressman Calls Firing Gay People One of the 'Freedoms We Enjoy'." *Daily Kos*, September 8, 2014. http://www.dailykos.com/story/2014/09/08/1328117/-GOP-congressman-calls-firing-gay-people-one-of-the-freedoms-we-enjoy.

Cobb, John B., Jr., ed. *Resistance: The New Role of Progressive Christians*. Louisville: Westminster John Knox Press, 2008.

"Compassion." Wikipedia, n.d., accessed August 5, 2018. https://en.wikipedia.org/wiki/Compassion.

Cornell University Public Policy Research Portal. "What Does the Scholarly Research Say about the Effects of

Discrimination on the Health of LGBT People?" Cornell University Public Policy Research Portal, 2019. https://whatweknow.inequality.cornell.edu/topics/lgbt-equality/what-does-scholarly-research-say-about-the-effects-of-discrimination-on-the-health-of-lgbt-people/.

Crossan, John Dominic. *The Power of Parable: How Fiction by Jesus Became Fiction about Jesus*. New York: HarperCollins, 2012.

Death Penalty Information Center. "Facts about the Death Penalty." Death Penalty Information Center, 2020. Retrieved from deathpenaltyinfo.org.

Desmond, Matthew. *Poverty, by America*. New York: Crown, 2023.

"The Disciples Prayer." Enfleshed, n.d., accessed December 10, 2022. https://enfleshed.com/liturgy/the-disciples-prayer/.

Ellison, Marvin M. *Erotic Justice: A Liberating Ethic of Sexuality*. Louisville: Westminster John Knox Press, 1996.

Ellison, Ralph. "Harlem is Nowhere." *Harper's Magazine*, August 8, 2014. https://harpers.org/archive/2014/08/harlem-is-nowhere-2/.

Faber, Jacob W. "Segregation and the Geography of Creditworthiness: Racial Inequality in a Recovered Mortgage Market." *Housing Policy Debate* 28, no. 2 (March 2018): 215–247.

Fletcher, Joseph. *Situation Ethics: The New Morality*. Philadelphia: The Westminster Press, 1966.

Gajewski, Misha. "We Still Think Brilliance Is a Male Trait and It's Hurting Women." *Forbes*, July 2, 2020. https://www.forbes.com/sites/mishagajewski/2020/07/02/we-still-think-that-brilliance-is-a-male-trait-and-this-is-hurting-women/?sh=486001fb452e.

Garcia, Emma. "Schools Are Still Segregated and Black Children are Paying a Price." Economic Policy Institute, February 12, 2020. https://www.epi.org/publication/

schools-are-still-segregated-and-black-children-are-paying-a-price/.

Geronimus, Arline T. *Weathering: The Extraordinary Stress of Ordinary Life in an Unjust Society*. New York: Little, Brown Spark, 2023.

Goosby, Bridget J., Jacob E. Cheadle, and Colter Mitchell. "Stress-Related Biosocial Mechanisms of Discrimination and African American Health Inequities." *Annual Review of Sociology* 44 (2018): 319–40.

Grundy, Christopher. *Recovering Communion in a Violent World: Resistance, Resilience, and Risk*. Eugene: Cascade Books, 2019.

Gulley, Phillip. *Unlearning God: How Unbelieving Helped Me Believe*. New York: Convergent Books, 2018.

Hamilton, Colleen. "How Drag Artists Became the Far Right's Ultimate Villains." *Them*, December 23, 2022. https://www.them.us/story/drag-gop-right-wing-attacks-explained.

Harnois, Catherine E., and João L. Bastos. "Discrimination, Harassment, and Gendered Health Inequalities: Do Perceptions of Workplace Mistreatment Contribute to the Gender Gap in Self-Reported Health?" *Journal of Health and Social Behavior* 59, no. 2 (June 2018): 283–99.

Hesse, Monica. "The One Point Abortion Rights Activists Need to Keep Making." *Washington Post*, October 3, 2022. https://www.washingtonpost.com/lifestyle/2022/10/03/abortion-rights-bodily-autonomy/.

Hillel International. "If I Am Not For Myself, Who Will Be For Me? A Discussion for Developing a Practice of Self-Care." Hillel International, February 28, 2017. https://www.hillel.org/if-i-am-not-for-myself-who-will-be-for-me-a-discussion-for-developing-a-practice-of-self-care/.

Johnson, Akilah. "Can Politics Kill You? Research Says the Answer Increasingly is Yes." *Washington Post*, December 16, 2022. https://www.washingtonpost.com/health/2022/12/16/politics-health-relationship/.

King, Martin Luther, Jr. *Where Do We Go From Here: Chaos or Community?* Boston: Beacon Press, 2010.

Kline, Patrick M., Evan K. Rose, and Christopher R. Walters. "Systemic Discrimination among Large U.S. Employers." National Bureau of Economic Research Working Paper, July 2021. https://www.nber.org/papers/w29053.

Korver-Glenn, Elizabeth. *Race Brokers: Housing Markets and Segregation in 21st Century Urban America*. New York: Oxford University Press, 2021.

Kuadli, Jennifer. "32 Shocking Sexual Assault Statistics for 2022." *LegalJobs*, January 18, 2022. https://legaljobs.io/blog/sexual-assault-statistics/.

Liptak, Adam, and Abbie VanSickle. "Supreme Court Backs Web Designer Opposed to Same-Sex Marriage." *New York Times*, June 30, 2023. https://www.nytimes.com/2023/06/30/us/supreme-court-same-sex-marriage.html.

"List of Mass Shootings in the United States in 2022." Wikipedia, n.d., accessed January 10, 2023. https://en.wikipedia.org/wiki/List_of_mass_shootings_in_the_United_States_in_2022.

Losen, Daniel J., and Paul Martinez. 2020. "Lost Opportunities: How Disparate School Discipline Continues to Drive Differences in the Opportunity to Learn." Learning Policy Institute, October 1, 2020. https://learningpolicyinstitute.org/product/crdc-school-discipline-report.

Mahowald, Lindsay, Sharita Gruberg, and John Halpin. "The State of the LGBTQ Community in 2020: A National Public Opinion Study." Center for American Progress, October 6, 2020. https://www.americanprogress.org/article/state-lgbtq-community-2020/.

McLaren, Brian D. *Do I Stay Christian? A Guide for the Doubters, the Disappointed, and the Disillusioned*. New York: St. Martin's, 2022.

Merton, Robert. "The Self-Fulfilling Prophecy." *The Antioch Review* 8, no. 2 (Summer 1948): 193-210.

National Partnership for Women & Families. "What's the Wage Gap in the States?" National Partnership for Women & Families, n.d., accessed December 28, 2022. https://www.nationalpartnership.org/our-work/economic-justice/wage-gap/#.

NBC News. "'Joe the Plumber' Pens 'Harsh' Open Letter to Isla Vista Relatives." NBC News, May 27, 2014. https://www.nbcnews.com/storyline/isla-vista-rampage/joe-plumber-pens-harsh-open-letter-isla-vista-relatives-n115561.

Ndulue, Ngozi. "Enduring Injustice: The Persistence of Racial Discrimination in the U.S. Death Penalty." Death Penalty Information Center, September 15, 2020. https://deathpenaltyinfo.org/facts-and-research/dpic-reports/in-depth/enduring-injustice-the-persistence-of-racial-discrimination-in-the-u-s-death-penalty.

Nelson, James B. *Embodiment: An Approach to Sexuality and Christian Theology.* Minneapolis: Augsburg Publishing House, 1978.

New Jersey Coalition against Sexual Assault. "Centering Bodily Autonomy in Conversations about Abortion." NJCASA, September 12, 2022. https://njcasa.org/news/centering-bodily-autonomy/.

Nochlin, Linda. "From 1971: Why Have There Been No Great Women Artists?" *ArtNews*, May 30, 2015. https://www.artnews.com/art-news/retrospective/why-have-there-been-no-great-women-artists-4201/.

Norman, Sonya B., and Shira Maguen. "Moral Injury." U.S. Department of Veterans Affairs, n.d.; accessed December 28, 2022. https://www.ptsd.va.gov/professional/treat/cooccurring/moral_injury.asp.

Oord, Thomas J. *Pluriform Love: An Open and Relational Theology of Well-Being.* Grasmere, ID: SacraSage, 2022.

Opotow, Susan. "Moral Exclusion and Injustice: An Introduction." *Journal of Social Issues* 46, no. 1 (Spring 1990): 1-20.

"Ordination of Women." Wikipedia, n.d., accessed December 28, 2022. https://en.wikipedia.org/wiki/Ordination_of_women.

Panza, Christopher, and Adam Potthast. *Ethics for Dummies*. Hoboken, NJ: Wiley Publishing, 2010.

Paul, Mark. *The Ends of Freedom: Reclaiming America's Lost Promise of Economic Rights*. Chicago: University of Chicago Press, 2023.

Pavlovitz, John. "Christians Are Supposed to Care about People." Stuff that Needs to Be Said, January 6, 2020. https://johnpavlovitz.com/2020/01/06/christians-are-supposed-to-care-about-people/.

Pavlovitz, John. *Hope and Other Superpowers: A Life-Affirming, Love-Defending, Butt-Kicking, World-Saving Manifesto*. New York: Simon & Schuster, 2018.

Peck, M. Scott. *The Road Less Traveled: A New Psychology of Love, Traditional Values, and Spiritual Growth*. New York: Simon & Schuster, 1978.

Penwell, Derek. *Outlandish: An Unlikely Messiah, a Messy Ministry, and the Call to Mobilize*. St. Louis: Chalice Press, 2018.

Phillips, Scott, and Justin Marceau. "Whom the State Kills." Social Science Research Network, July 30, 2020. https://papers.ssrn.com/sol3/papers.cfm?abstract_id=3440828.

Porterfield, Jason. *Fight Like Jesus: How Jesus Waged Peace throughout Holy Week*. Harrisburg, VA: Herald Press, 2022.

Powers, Kirsten. *Saving Grace: Speak Your Truth, Stay Centered, and Learn to Coexist with People Who Drive You Nuts*. New York: Convergent Books, 2021.

ProgressiveChristianity.org. "2022 Version of the Core Values of Progressive Christianity." ProgressiveChristianity.org, n.d., accessed January 7, 2023. https://progressivechristianity.org/the-8-points/.

Quadlin, Natasha. "The Mark of a Woman's Record: Gender and Academic Performance in Hiring," *American Sociological Review* 83, no. 2 (April 2018): 331–360.

Rooney, Emma. "The Effects of Sexual Objectification on Women's Mental Health." *Applied Psychology Opus*, n.d., accessed May 13, 2021. https://wp.nyu.edu/steinhardt-appsych_opus/the-effects-of-sexual-objectification-on-womens-mental-health/.

Ross, Loretta J. "What If We Called People In, Rather than Calling Them Out?" NPR, December 3, 2021. https://www.npr.org/2021/12/03/1061209084/loretta-j-ross-what-if-we-called-people-in-rather-than-calling-them-out.

Rothstein, Richard. *The Color of Law: A Forgotten History of How Our Government Segregated America*. New York: Liveright Publishing, 2017.

Ruttenberg, Danya. *On Repentance and Repair: Making Amends in an Unapologetic World*. Boston: Beacon Press, 2022.

Sayer, Andrew. *Why Things Matter to People: Social Science, Values, and Ethical Life*. New York: Cambridge University Press, 2011.

"Second Bill of Rights." Wikipedia, n.d., accessed December 7, 2022. https://en.wikipedia.org/wiki/Second_Bill_of_Rights.

Sima, Richard. "Racism Takes a Toll on the Brain, Research Shows." *Washington Post*, February 16, 2023. https://www.washingtonpost.com/wellness/2023/02/16/racism-brain-mental-health-impact/.

Simons, Ronald L., Man-Kit Lei, Steven R. Beach, Ashley B. Barr, Leslie G. Simons, and Frederick X. Gibbons. "Discrimination, Segregation, and Chronic Inflammation: Testing the Weathering Explanation for the Poor Health of Black Americans." *Developmental Psychology*

54, no. 10 (October 2018): 1993–2006.

Singletary, Michelle. "Shopping While Black. African Americans Continue to Face Retail Racism." *Washington Post*, May 17, 2018. https://www.washingtonpost.com/news/get-there/wp/2018/05/17/shopping-while-black-african-americans-continue-to-face-retail-racism/.

Smith, Emily Esfahani. *The Power of Meaning: Finding Fulfillment in a World Obsessed with Happiness*. New York: Broadway Books, 2017.

Solzhenitsyn, Aleksandr. *The Gulag Archipelago, Volume Two*. New York: Harper & Row, 1975.

Steele, Claude M. *Whistling Vivaldi: How Stereotypes Affect Us and What We Can Do*. New York: W.W. Norton, 2010.

Struckmeyer, Kurt. *A Conspiracy of Love: Following Jesus in a Postmodern World*. Eugene, OR: Resource Publications, 2016.

Struckmeyer, Kurt. *An Unorthodox Faith: A New Reformation for a Postmodern World*. Eugene, OR: Resource Publications, 2017.

Tatter, Grace. "Achieving King's Beloved Community." Harvard Graduate School of Education, January 18, 2019. https://www.gse.harvard.edu/news/19/01/achieving-kings-beloved-community.

Trevor Project, The. "The Trevor Project 2022 National Survey on LGBTQ Youth Mental Health." The Trevor Project, 2022. https://www.thetrevorproject.org/survey-2022/.

Tuerkheimer, Deborah. *Credible: Why We Doubt Accusers and Protect Abusers*. New York: HarperCollins, 2021.

University of California San Diego Center on Gender Equity and Health/Stop Street Harassment. 2019. "Measuring #MeToo: A National Study on Sexual Harassment and Assault." UCSDCGEH/Stop Street Harassment, April 2019. https://www.raliance.org/report_posts/measuring-metoo-a-national-study-on-sexual-harassment-and-assault/.

Valenti, Jessica. *He's a Stud, She's a Slut and 49 Other Double Standards Every Woman Should Know.* Berkeley, CA: Seal Press, 2008.

Villarosa, Linda. *Under the Skin: The Hidden Toll of Racism on American Lives and on the Health of Our Nation.* New York: Doubleday, 2022.

West, Cornel. *The American Evasion of Philosophy: A Genealogy of Pragmatism.* Madison: University of Wisconsin Press, 1989.

Zuckerman, Phil. *Living the Secular Life: New Answers to Old Questions.* New York: Penguin Press, 2014.